Have a Ball!

Basketball is a great game—to play, to watch, to talk about. It's a thrill-a-minute from the first dunk to the final buzzer. It's your favorite team fighting to make the playoffs and win the gold ring in the NBA Finals.

It's a made-in-America sport that began with a peach basket more than 100 years ago and today is an international game played and followed by millions the world over.

The NBA Book of Fantastic Facts, Feats & Super Stats is a bottomless basket of information. From amazing stories and quick quizzes to player profiles . . . from incredible performances and unmatched records to odd lists and facts about the NBA's Olympic Dream Teams . . . the book is designed to be a slam dunk.

1996 EDITION

The NBA

Book

of Fantastic Facts, Feats & Super Stats

The NBA Book of Fantastic Facts, Feats & Super Stats

1996 EDITION

Edited by Zander Hollander

Rainbow Bridge®

Troll

Copyright © 1996 by NBA Properties, Inc.
The NBA and NBA Team insignia reproduced within this book are the exclusive property of NBA Properties, Inc. and the respective NBA teams and are used herein under license from NBA Properties, Inc.

Published by Rainbow Bridge, an imprint and trademark of Troll Communications L.L.C.

Printed in the United States of America.

10 9 8 7 6 5 4 3 2 1

Photo Credits
Cover: Nathaniel S. Butler, NBA Photos
Muggsy Bogues/Gregg Forwerck, NBA Photos
Michael Jordan/Andrew D. Bernstein, NBA Photos
Gary Payton/Scott Cunningham, NBA Photos
Grant Hill/Nathaniel S. Butler, NBA Photos
Charles Barkley/Andrew Bernstein, NBA Photos
Jason Kidd/Gregg Forwerck, NBA Photos
Alonzo Mourning/Dale Tait, NBA Photos
David Robinson and Karl Malone/Chris Covatta, NBA Photos

Contents

— — —

Hakeem Olajuwon, David Robinson, John
Stockton, Charles Barkley, Joe Dumars, Jason
Kidd, Dennis Rodman, Karl Malone, Reggie
Miller, Shawn Kemp, Grant Hill, Nick Van Exel,
Mookie Blaylock, Patrick Ewing, Glen Rice,
Rod Strickland, Clifford Robinson, Dikembe
Mutombo, Dana Barros, Jamal Mashburn,
Latrell Sprewell, Glenn Robinson, Chris
Webber, Scottie Pippen, Alonzo Mourning, Brad
Daugherty, Kevin Johnson, Tim Hardaway,
Mahmoud Abdul-Rauf, Otis Thorpe, Mitch
Richmond, Larry Johnson, Kenny Anderson,
Mark Price, Gary Payton, Shawn Bradley, Jim
Jackson, Vlade Divac

Acknowledgments

Canadian-born Doc Naismith would have especially welcomed the 1995-1996 NBA season. If he were alive, the man who invented basketball would have brought his peach basket to the opening games of the Toronto Raptors and Vancouver Grizzlies, the newest teams in the NBA.

Naismith envisioned basketball as a game any number of people could play. As editor of this second edition of *The NBA Book of Fantastic Facts, Feats & Super Stats*, I proceeded along the same lines, although all was not play. There were many who aided in the research and writing of the book.

I acknowledge in particular contributing editor Eric Compton, who led our team in assists, and writers Fred Kerber of the *New York Post*, Scott Howard-Cooper of the *Los Angeles Times*, and David Kaplan of the *New York Daily News*.

Also Bob Rosen of Elias Sports Bureau, Lee Stowbridge, movie maven Jeffrey Lyons, Phyllis Hollander of Associated Features, Chip Lovitt, Carol Anderson, and Eileen Turano of Troll Communications, the Basketball Hall of Fame's Wayne Patterson, the NBA's Frank Fochetta, Diane Naughton, Clare Martin, NBA Photos, and the league and team public relations directors.

Many sources were used, including eyewitnesses, interviews, newspapers, magazines, Associated Features books, and *The Official NBA Basketball Encyclopedia*.

Zander Hollander

Shaq & Penny: Hit Show From the Magic Kingdom

They're a dynamic duo. They're different in almost every way. Shaquille Rashaun O'Neal is 7'1", 303 pounds. Anfernee (Penny) Hardaway is 6'7", 200 pounds. Shaq raps, Penny plays cool. But together, they are the heart and excitement of the Orlando Magic.

They grew up worlds apart. Shaq, the son of a strict U.S. Army sergeant, was born March 6, 1972, in Newark, New Jersey. From ages 12 to 15 he lived on military bases in Germany. Penny, an only child raised by his grandmother, was born July 18, 1972, in Memphis, Tennessee.

Louise Hardaway called her grandson "Pretty" when he was a toddler, but something got lost in the translation. Everybody thought she was calling him "Penny." And that's been his nickname ever since.

Shaq was 6'7" by the time he was 14 and was so clumsy he couldn't even dunk. He had grown too fast and was hampered by Osgood-Schlatter's disease, which caused discomfort in his knees.

Penny was tall for his age—6'4" as a 12-year-old— so basketball was an ideal sport to pursue. "The game was easy for him," said Jim Kern, his coach at the

Memphis YMCA. "He wasn't like most kids his size. He was coordinated, could run, handle the ball, score, rebound, do anything. We didn't call him a guard, forward, or center. We just put him out there and said, 'Go.' He made things happen."

At Robert Cole High School in San Antonio, Texas, which had an army base, Shaq became a one-man army. He led his team to a 68–1 record, prompting a flock of college coaches to recruit him. Shaq settled on Louisiana State.

Shaq and Penny have known each other since they met at the Olympic Festival in 1989. "I was in high school (Treadwell in Memphis) and he was a sophomore in college," Penny said. "Our rooms were across the hall from each other. The way we played together then, he wanted me to come to LSU. We always had this certain thing for each other on the court. We clicked from the beginning."

Penny went on to a glorious career at Memphis State, where they saluted him by retiring his number, 25. He was selected by the Golden State Warriors with the third pick in the 1993 Draft but was immediately traded to the Magic, along with three draft picks, for No. 1 pick Chris Webber.

Shaq left LSU after his junior year as a two-time All-American and was the No. 1 pick by the Magic in 1992. He became the NBA's thunder-dunking man-child and was named Rookie of the Year in 1992-93. Shaq cut an awesome figure—never more so than when crashing the boards with his arena-rattling dunks. With his affable personality and exuberant smile, he became an overnight sensation creating "Shaq Mania" everywhere he went.

This all set the stage for Penny's arrival in 1993-94. And what a season it was for this combo! Penny led all rookies in steals and assists, and made the All-Rookie First Team. Shaq averaged 29.3 points a game, losing the scoring title only after San Antonio's David Robinson scored 71 points on the final day of the season. And in the summer of '94 he dominated the World Championship of Basketball as the leader of the USA Dream Team II.

Shaq and Penny had another spectacular season in 1994-95. Shaq led the league in scoring, was second in shooting percentage, third in rebounds, and sixth in blocks. Penny averaged 20.9 points and won praise for his boundless all-around skills. And he was named to the All-NBA First Team.

But the Magic were swept by the Houston Rockets in the NBA Finals.

That was the singular frustration in a season that saw Shaq as busy as ever, cutting rap records and playing pitchman for all sorts of products.

Penny's appeal is greater than ever, but in no way comparable to Shaq's. Does it bother Penny? "No way at all," he says. "I don't worry about those things. I just want to win. That's all I worry about. We're both very unselfish. We both want to see the other do well."

Hardaway

Year	Team	G	FG	FG Pct.	FT	FT Pct.	Reb.	Ast.	TP	Avg.
1993-94	Orlando	82	509	.466	245	.742	439	544	1313	16.0
1994-95	Orlando	77	585	.512	356	.769	336	551	1613	20.9
	Totals	159	1094	.490	601	.758	775	1095	2926	18.4
Playoff Totals		24	166	.468	91	.752	99	183	468	19.5

O'Neal

Year	Team	G	FG	FG Pct.	FT	FT Pct.	Reb.	Ast.	TP	Avg.
1992-93	Orlando	81	733	.562	427	.592	1122	152	1893	23.4
1993-94	Orlando	81	953	.599	471	.554	1072	195	2377	29.3
1994-95	Orlando	79	930	.583	455	.533	901	214	2315	29.3
	Totals	241	2616	.583	1353	.558	3095	561	6585	27.3
Playoff Totals		24	218	.569	165	.559	290	77	601	25.0

Michael Jordan's Greatest Moments

Where does he go from here? How about quarterback in the NFL? Hockey? Tennis? Baseball didn't work, but there has to be another goal for Michael Jeffrey Jordan, who lives for new challenges.

It has been that way from the earliest days of basketball's most celebrated player, who was born February 16, 1963, in Brooklyn, New York, and grew up in Wilmington, North Carolina.

So what's next? For now it is his usual artistry as "Air Jordan," tongue hanging out as he makes one electrifying shot after another before sellout crowds and millions of television viewers.

Whether he's making a new movie, as he did with Bugs Bunny in *Space Jam*, a new commercial, or playing the game he loves best, the most famous Bull of all continues to seek perfection. And that can only mean more momentous feats in his legendary career.

What follows are his "Greatest Moments" to date. There's no question that he'll be adding new ones in the course of the 1995-96 season.

March 29, 1982—It was only the beginning for the freshman at the University of North Carolina. Michael hits a game-winning 17-foot jumper with 17 seconds left to beat Georgetown, 63–62, for the NCAA crown.

"That shot put me on the basketball map," said Michael.

April 21, 1986—Michael had sat out 64 games during the regular season with a broken foot. But the bounding Bull is at his peak against the Celtics in Game 2 of the first round of the NBA playoffs at Boston Garden. He scores an NBA playoff-record 63 points in a double-overtime game won by Boston, 135–131.

"I had missed so many games that year and was anxious to come back and show that I was healed. I like accepting challenges and proving people wrong," said Michael.

November 21, 1986—Michael scores the Bulls' final 18 points in a 101–99 victory over the Knicks at Chicago Stadium. He has 40 points for the night.

April 16, 1987—Michael sets an NBA record with 23 consecutive points against the Hawks at Chicago Stadium. He had a total of 61 points, but Atlanta wins, 117–114.

February 7, 1988—After dazzling a partisan crowd at Chicago Stadium with his acrobatic moves to win the Slam-Dunk Championship, Michael tosses in 40 points to lead the East to a 138–133 victory over the West in the All-Star Game. He seals the MVP award when he notches 16 points in the last six minutes.

May 7, 1989—Cleveland fans will forever refer to it as "The Shot." They'll never get over Michael's jumper from the key at the buzzer that gives the visiting Bulls a 101–100 victory and the series in the first round of the playoffs.

March 28, 1990—Michael flies to a career-high 69 points in an overtime win, 117–113, against the Cavaliers. He is 23 for 37 from the field and sinks 21 of 23 free throws. And he bags a career-high 18 rebounds.

"It was just one of those games where I felt rhythm from the beginning," said Michael. "I felt like I couldn't miss. The best part is that we won the game."

June 12, 1991—The Bulls beat the Lakers to win their first NBA Championship as Michael scores 30 points and dishes out 10 assists in Game 5 at The Forum. The regular-season MVP, he's also named playoff MVP, and, clutching his trophy, he weeps unashamedly.

"I've never been this emotional in public, but I couldn't help myself," said Michael. "Winning the championship has capped it all for me. It ended seven years of waiting."

June 3, 1992—Michael explodes for 35 points in the first half for a playoff record against the Trail Blazers in Game 1 of the NBA Finals at Chicago Stadium. Jordan also ties a record by making six 3-pointers in the half.

"I came out very relaxed tonight and it just flowed," said Michael. "It seemed like the hoop was six feet wide. Every shot felt easier than a free throw."

June 14, 1992—Trailing Portland by 15 points going into the final quarter of Game 6 of the NBA Finals,

Michael and his Bulls come back to win, 97–93, for their second straight title. Michael gets his second Finals MVP award and celebrates with the Chicago Stadium crowd by dancing on the scorers' table.

"We couldn't have done this without the support of our fans," said Michael. "That's why we came back on the court to salute them."

May 17, 1993—With Gerald Wilkins' hand in his face, and Cleveland fans booing him loudly, Michael nets an 18-footer as the clock runs out at Richfield Coliseum. The shot beats the Cavaliers, 103–101, and completes a sweep in the Eastern Conference semifinals.

"It was nice to do it in front of the Cleveland fans," said Michael. "I got the final word. There was never a doubt the shot wouldn't go in."

June 20, 1993—Michael is NBA Finals MVP again as the Bulls win their third straight title, defeating Phoenix, 99–98, in Game 6 at America West Arena. Michael's 41-point average in the Finals is a record.

"Winning this championship was harder than anything I've ever done in basketball," said Michael. "I did something Larry [Bird] and Magic [Johnson] didn't do: Win three in a row. That's something I can tell my grandkids about."

March 28, 1995—In only his fifth NBA game since returning to the sport, Michael delivers a sparkling 55-point performance against the Knicks at Madison Square Garden. Thirty-five of his points come in the first half as he shows everybody that he is still the Michael of old. And it is his pass for the winning basket with 3.1 seconds left that wraps up the Bulls' 113–111 victory.

Former Knick Earl Monroe said, "It was like he never left. It's like he made two years disappear."

Said Michael: "That's the fun of it. Tomorrow you don't know what I might do."

Year	Team	G	FG	FG Pct.	FT	FT Pct.	Reb.	Ast.	TP	Avg.
1984-85	Chicago	82	837	.515	630	.845	534	481	2313	28.2
1985-86	Chicago	18	150	.457	105	.840	64	53	408	22.7
1986-87	Chicago	82	1098	.482	833	.857	430	377	3041	37.1
1987-88	Chicago	82	1069	.535	723	.841	449	485	2868	35.0
1988-89	Chicago	81	966	.538	674	.850	652	650	2633	32.5
1989-90	Chicago	82	1034	.526	593	.848	565	519	2753	33.6
1990-91	Chicago	82	990	.539	571	.851	492	453	2580	31.5
1991-92	Chicago	80	943	.519	491	.832	511	489	2404	30.1
1992-93	Chicago	78	992	.495	476	.837	522	428	2541	32.6
1994-95	Chicago	17	166	.411	109	.801	117	90	457	26.9
Totals		684	8245	.514	5205	.845	4336	4025	21998	32.2
Playoff Totals		121	1531	.499	1006	.833	806	783	4165	34.4

Clyde Drexler
Took Off Like a Rocket

The setting was The Summit in Houston, just after the Rockets had swept Orlando in Game 4 of the 1995 NBA Finals. It was the night of June 14 and the scene in the Rockets' arena was a wild one.

More than anyone else, Clyde Drexler had reason to do handstands and leap to the sky. Instead, "Clyde the Glide" simply embraced his MVP teammate Hakeem Olajuwon and settled for a high-five that said it all, for both their long friendship and Drexler's first championship ring.

After 12 years, $10\frac{1}{2}$ of which had been marked by his role as a superstar with the Portland Trail Blazers, Drexler had made a sensational return to his hometown. He and Olajuwon had led the University of Houston's "Phi Slama Jama" gang to the NCAA Final Four in 1982. Then they reached the 1983 NCAA Championship Finals in Albuquerque, New Mexico, only to be upset by North Carolina State.

Houston fans will never get over that one, but that's ancient history. And if anything can ease those memories, Clyde Drexler's contributions to the Rockets' second championship season in a row certainly will.

When the Rockets were on the verge of being eliminated by the Utah Jazz in the fifth and deciding game of the first round of the playoffs, Drexler made the difference. Suddenly he was everywhere, making steals, getting big rebounds, and leading the charge on the fastbreak as the Rockets came back to win.

"When Clyde takes the rebound, puts his head down, and takes off, he's like a thoroughbred, and he makes you run with him," said teammate Mario Elie. "It's like he's 10 years younger, flying by young guys like they're standing still."

The 6'7", 225-pound guard was born June 22, 1962, in New Orleans. One of seven children, he grew up in Houston, where he began playing high school basketball as a junior and made all-city as a 6'6" senior.

At the University of Houston, Drexler became the school's first player to score 1,000 points, snag 900 rebounds, and earn 300 assists in a career.

The Trail Blazers drafted him 14th in 1983 and he soon became one of the league's most dominant players. He played in eight All-Star Games and led Portland to two NBA Finals. He made the All-NBA First Team in 1991-92 and played on the gold-medal Dream Team in the 1992 Olympic Games in Barcelona, Spain.

On Valentine's Day, 1995, Drexler was traded to the Rockets with Tracy Murray for Otis Thorpe and the rights to Marcelo Nicola. He gave the Rockets a vital new offensive weapon.

"He came in here and told me, 'I just want to fit in.' And that's what he did," said teammate Elie. "He became the leader out there. Always positive, never negative."

It all paid off for Houston and "Clyde the Glide."

Year	Team	G	FG	FG Pct.	FT	FT Pct.	Reb.	Ast.	TP	Avg.
1983-84	Portland	82	252	.451	123	.728	235	153	628	7.7
1984-85	Portland	80	573	.494	223	.759	476	441	1377	17.2
1985-86	Portland	75	542	.475	293	.769	421	600	1389	18.5
1986-87	Portland	82	707	.502	357	.760	518	566	1782	21.7
1987-88	Portland	81	849	.506	476	.811	533	467	2185	27.0
1988-89	Portland	78	829	.496	438	.799	615	450	2123	27.2
1989-90	Portland	73	670	.494	333	.774	507	432	1703	23.3
1990-91	Portland	82	645	.482	416	.794	546	493	1767	21.5
1991-92	Portland	76	694	.470	401	.794	500	512	1903	25.0
1992-93	Portland	49	350	.429	245	.839	309	278	976	19.9
1993-94	Portland	68	473	.428	286	.777	445	333	1303	19.2
1994-95	Portland-Houston	76	571	.461	364	.824	480	362	1653	21.8
	Totals	902	7155	.479	3955	.789	5585	5087	18789	20.8
	Playoff Totals	116	901	.455	574	.791	824	751	2465	21.3

Kevin Garnett:
From High School to the Pros

— — —

"Millions of kids want to play pro basketball and here I am getting the chance early," said 19-year-old Kevin Garnett.

How early is it? Very early. He only attended his senior prom in May 1995. Selected by the Minnesota Timberwolves as the fifth pick in the 1995 NBA Draft, Garnett became one of only five players in NBA history to enter the league without having played in college.

No rookie would be followed more closely in 1995-96 than the 6'10", 220-pound forward from South Carolina.

Who is Kevin Garnett to defy custom and take the shortest route to a career in the pros?

He was born May 19, 1976, in Mauldin, South Carolina, and he was named the state's "Mr. Basketball" as a junior at Mauldin High. At a summer basketball camp in 1994, he met Bill Nelson, coach of Chicago's Farragut Academy, and made the switch that would soon lead to the NBA. Kevin and his mother, Shirley, moved to Chicago, where he enrolled at Farragut for his senior year in 1994-95.

There he averaged 25.2 points, 17.9 rebounds, 6.7 assists, and 6.5 blocks while shooting 60 percent from the field. And the NBA scouts were watching him. Kevin could hit 20-foot jumpers and proved to be a tremendous leaper, smooth ball-handler, and clever passer. That all added up to his being named National High School Player of the Year by *USA Today* and making *Parade Magazine's* All-American team.

The next step would have been college, and Kevin was sought by a number of schools. But when he didn't qualify for a Division I scholarship, he decided to declare himself available for the NBA Draft. Representatives of more than a dozen NBA teams watched him in workouts at the University of Illinois-Chicago. And most of them came away feeling that Kevin had the right stuff.

Sure, he's a boy in a man's world. He needs to develop physically so he can match up against players who are older, stronger, and more experienced.

By now, Kevin has read all about the careers of the other schoolboys who made it into the pros from high school—Moses Malone, Darryl Dawkins, Bill Willoughby, and Shawn Kemp. They did it. Why can't he?

Minnesota realistically can't expect him to be a super-Wolf in his first season. He has a lot of learning and adjusting ahead. But as Kevin wrote to NBA Commissioner David Stern before the draft: "I know I will be among the finest players in the world."

NBA
Special-lists!
— — —

Fred Kerber follows basketball around the clock and around the land for the *New York Post*. Between baskets, he likes to make lists. Basketball lists. What follows are samples of Kerber running the court.

Good Things,
Small Packages

You don't have to be big to be a basketball star. Honest. Oh, it helps to be 7 feet tall and have trouble finding clothes that fit. But the smaller guys can make an impact, too. Just ask any opponent who ever tried to stop Isiah Thomas, the ex-Piston who is now vice president of the Toronto Raptors. And there are plenty of good little men still playing.

1. Tyrone "Muggsy" Bogues, Charlotte—He's only 5'3". The shortest player ever in the NBA.
2. Anthony "Spud" Webb, Atlanta—Ever hear of a Slam-Dunk champion who's only 5'7"? This guy beat out all the big guys on All-Star Weekend in 1986.
3. Dana Barros, Boston—It doesn't matter how tall you are when you can shoot like this 5'11" marksman.

4. John Stockton, Utah—The greatest assist man. Not even Magic Johnson passed for as many assists as this 6'1" leader now seeking his ninth straight assists crown.

5. Mookie Blaylock, Atlanta—Just watch any of the big guys get frustrated trying to bring the ball past this ferocious 6'1" defender.

6. Kenny Anderson, New Jersey—Many said he was too small to play in the pros. But now they're saying this 6'1" Nets star is among the most creative players in the game.

7. Elliot Perry, Phoenix—When you're only an even 6 feet, you have to have heart. And even after some teams told him he couldn't play, he kept trying. He was a big reason for the Suns' success in 1994-95.

8. Terrell Brandon, Cleveland—Cavs fans realized how important this 6-foot guard was after he was injured in 1994-95. They realized it even when he took over for the traded Mark Price.

9. Dee Brown, Boston—When you're 6'1", it helps to have rocket boosters in your socks like this flying Celtic.

10. Nick Van Exel, L.A. Lakers—Some teams look mighty foolish for having passed on this 6'1" dynamo in the 1993 Draft.

11. Avery Johnson, San Antonio—Another never-say-die guy. This 5'11" sparkplug bounced around the league and the Continental Basketball Association for seven years, then helped the Spurs to the Western Conference Finals in 1994-95.

It's What They Say and How They Say It

Some players are always in the news. They're famous for their play. Or they get noticed for some of the things they say. Reporters around the league always seek out certain guys because they seem to have the answers—funny answers, insightful answers—right at the tips of their tongues. There are a number of such players. Here are some of the best.

1. Charles Barkley, Phoenix—He always says what's on his mind.
2. Glenn "Doc" Rivers, San Antonio—The reporters always flock to Doc. He's smart, warm, and funny.
3. Grant Hill, Detroit—His mother's college roommate was Hillary Clinton. His dad went to Yale and was a football star with the Dallas Cowboys. And now he's the star of the family.
4. David Robinson, San Antonio—You've seen "The Admiral" play basketball. You should hear the great advice he gives to kids.
5. Joe Dumars, Detroit—He grew up in a small Louisiana town and has never let his stardom affect his small-town charm or wisdom.
6. Reggie Miller, Indiana—He says things that often make other players angry. But he gets the advantage when they lose their cool.
7. Avery Johnson, San Antonio—There must be something in the San Antonio water. Here is another affable, sincere fellow who always has time for fans and reporters.

8. Buck Williams, Portland—He's such a gifted speaker and smart man that the players elected him to be president of their union.
9. Derek Harper, New York—He'll answer all your questions about basketball. But what he loves to talk about most are his kids.
10. Michael Jordan, Chicago—When you're in demand the way he is, people always want to hear what you have to say.

Unforgettable

Some players, such as Michael Jordan, are unforgettable for the way they play. You watch them dunk a basketball, and the image lasts forever. But some NBA players are memorable for other reasons, such as their hair, their clothes, or some other characteristic.

1. Dennis Rodman, Chicago—Just check out his hair to see what the color of the week is. That is, if you can take your eyes off his body tattoos.

2. Anthony Mason, New York—He shaves messages into the side of his scalp. Think of the money he could make renting out advertising space.

3. Shaquille O'Neal, Orlando—There is simply no way to ignore a man who is 7'1", weighs over 300 pounds, and plays with his quickness.

4. Gheorghe Muresan, Washington—Here's another player whose sheer size (7'7") makes him unforgettable. He makes 7-foot Patrick Ewing look tiny.

5. Charles Barkley, Phoenix—One of the league's funniest players, at least with his comments. Once he's on the court, he is all business.

6. Tim Hardaway, Golden State—You can't say that fame has affected him. When he was serving as a TV interviewer during the playoffs, he started his analysis with, "Yo, man."

7. Bill Fitch, L.A. Clippers—Okay, he's a coach, not a player. But when his team was in a bad losing streak in 1994-95, he advised his players to only go shopping once a week. "That way, the fans will boo you only once a week outside the arena," he explained.

8. Charles Oakley, New York—Take one look at the color of his suits—he designs his own clothing—and you'll know why he's on this list. You need sunglasses to view his apparel.

9. Larry Johnson, Charlotte—Yes, he's a terrific player. And he always looks like he's having so much fun on the court.

10. John Salley, Toronto—He's just plain funny. He's actually done some gigs as a stand-up comedian.

Ten Great Places to See an NBA Game

You've saved up your money and gone out and bought tickets to an NBA game. But the game itself is only part of the fun. Where you watch it has a lot to do with it. There are simply some places to watch a game that are better than others. Two great buildings, Chicago Stadium and Boston Garden, have been torn down recently to make room for new arenas. But there are still plenty of great places to watch NBA action.

1. Madison Square Garden, New York—They call basketball "The City Game," and New York is the city they mean. And for a mere $1,000, you can sit at courtside next to Spike Lee.

2. America West Arena, Phoenix—There is hardly a bad seat in the house. And the gorilla is always entertaining, even if the game isn't.

3. Gund Arena, Cleveland—Another modern building with a great view of the game from all seats. Also, the food is better than at most other arenas.

4. Orlando Arena, Orlando—If you come to the O-Rena and don't have a good time, something's wrong. The fans are wild (even if they sometimes cheer and boo at the wrong time), and the seats are good.

5. The Great Western Forum, Los Angeles—It's starting to show its age, but when the Lakers are winning, it's a great place for fans. When the Lakers win, Hollywood's movie stars come out to watch the action.

6. Reunion Arena, Dallas—Another place that really rocks during the good times. It also has good sight-lines for the fans.

7. Bradley Center, Milwaukee—It's relatively new, but it's not huge and doesn't make you feel like you've crossed the state if you walk from one end to the other. The food is good, too.

8. The Palace of Auburn Hills, Detroit—So it takes half a day just to say the name of the place. And it's not the most conveniently located spot. But the seats, the food, and the fans are top-notch.

9. ARCO Arena, Sacramento—They plopped the building in the middle of nowhere, about five miles from Where-are-we. But the fans love the modern facility and it has one of the better gift shops.

10. Market Square Arena, Indiana—Not the favorite spot for players, who often complain about the lighting. But the fans rarely complain about the downtown facility—unless the Pacers lose, of course.

Out of Nowhere

Not every NBA player was a major star in college. And not every player went to a big-name school with television exposure. Some attended places you've probably never heard about. Some played in places all over the world. Some of them, in a sense, simply came out of nowhere. Here are a few of those guys.

1. John Starks, New York—A few years before he was playing for the Knicks, he was bagging groceries back home in Oklahoma.
2. John Stockton, Utah—He went to Gonzaga College, and when he was drafted by the Jazz, some people couldn't remember if he was John Stockton from Gonzaga or John Gonzaga from Stockton. They remember now.
3. Anthony Mason, New York—He once played in Turkey. He said he'll never fear a trade because "there's no place farther away than Turkey that they can send me."
4. Avery Johnson, San Antonio—He came out of Southern University in Louisiana and wasn't even drafted. And for years, he always was just about to make it. Finally, he has made it big.
5. Scottie Pippen, Chicago—It seems hard to believe that one of the game's greatest players was a virtual college unknown until his senior year at Central Arkansas.
6. David Benoit, Utah—Here's another player who was undrafted out of college. But he went on to be a starting forward on a team that won 60 games in 1994-95.

7. Antonio Davis, Indiana—He was the 15th player drafted in 1990 out of Texas-El Paso. There are a lot of NBA teams now asking for a do-over on that draft.

8. Joe Dumars, Detroit—He's from McNeese State, and although the Pistons thought he'd be good, no one ever thought he'd be THAT good.

9. Cedric Ceballos, L.A. Lakers—Phoenix always has a knack for finding good players in the second round. And this guy has turned out to be one of the best finds. He was the 48th player taken, out of Cal State–Fullerton, in 1990.

10. Vlade Divac, L.A. Lakers—Oh, the pro scouts knew about this European star. But only the Lakers were smart enough to draft him late in the first round in 1989.

11. Chris Dudley, Portland—Yale men aren't supposed to make good NBA players. But this center, who lasted until the 75th pick in the fourth round in 1987, has proven that theory wrong.

12. Mario Elie, Houston—A seventh-round pick in 1985 out of American International. Well, this seventh-round pick has two championship rings.

No Titles Without Teamwork

Teamwork. That's what brings championships. NBA history is filled with great individual players who never realized their dream of winning an NBA title. And even some of the greatest, such as Kareem Abdul-Jabbar and Michael Jordan, didn't get their rings until they got enough help. So, in no particular order, here are some of the teams generally regarded among the best ever in the NBA.

1. Lakers, 1971-72—This bunch, with Hall of Famers Jerry West, Wilt Chamberlain, and Elgin Baylor, won a record 33 games in a row on the way to a record 69 victories.
2. Knicks, 1969-70—With Willis Reed, Bill Bradley, Dave DeBusschere, Walt Frazier, and Dick Barnett, this team is still regarded as the ultimate model for passing and teamwork.
3. Bulls, 1991-92—After threatening to win 70 games—they won 67—the Bulls, with Michael Jordan, Scottie Pippen, and Horace Grant, breezed to the second of three straight titles, losing only four games in the entire playoffs.
4. Celtics, 1985-86—What was the best Celtic team ever? That's almost impossible to say, but this bunch, with Larry Bird, Robert Parish, and Kevin McHale up front, and Bill Walton in reserve, might have been the best Boston has seen.
5. 76ers, 1966-67—With Wilt Chamberlain dominating in the middle, the Sixers won 68 games and lost only two at home.
6. Celtics, 1961-62—The roster of this 60-victory

championship team reads likes a "Who's Who" in Celtic tradition: Bill Russell, Bob Cousy, K.C. Jones, Sam Jones, Frank Ramsey, Tom Heinsohn, and Tom Sanders.

7. Pistons, 1988-89—These were the original "Bad Boys," defensive monsters who changed the direction of the game. They were the masters of the 7-point blowout.

8. Lakers, 1986-87—There were a host of great Laker teams in the 1980s. And this was just one of them, with Magic Johnson, Kareem Abdul-Jabbar, Byron Scott, and James Worthy, among others.

9. Rockets, 1994-95—No team ever won fewer games in the regular season (47) and still won an NBA championship. They deserve inclusion among the greatest teams because they won their title with a display of teamwork that swept the favored Orlando Magic.

10. Bucks, 1970-71—Kareem Abdul-Jabbar needed only two seasons to win his first NBA championship. But he also needed the help that was supplied when the Bucks added Oscar Robertson, one of the greatest ever, to the roster.

Yo, NBA Raps!

Players do have lives beyond basketball. They have hobbies. They collect things. They go places. They even sing. Some of them, such as Shaquille O'Neal and Wayman Tisdale, do it professionally. By now everyone knows Shaq is a rapper. But other guys rap or play instruments, too. So an All-NBA rap 'n' roll band might look something like this:

1. Shaquille O'Neal, Orlando—Vocals. The world's most famous 7'1", 303-pound rapper.
2. Wayman Tisdale, Phoenix—Guitar, vocals. He carries a bass guitar on the road with him.
3. David Robinson, San Antonio—Sax and keyboard. Or anything he wants.
4. Terry Cummings, San Antonio—Keyboard, vocals. No outrageous songs, though. He's also an ordained minister.
5. Grant Hill, Detroit—Keyboard. You get the feeling this guy can do just about anything.
6. Horace Grant, Orlando—Vocals. Probably backup vocals. This all-star has always been the missing piece to great teams in Chicago and Orlando.
7. Dennis Rodman, Chicago—Vocals. Backed up by his mynah bird.
8. Reggie Miller, Indiana—Vocals. He's got to be a good rapper. He never shuts up.
9. Dana Barros, Boston—Vocals. At 5'11", he'll hit all the low notes.
10. Tony Lavelli, Celtics (1949-50), Knicks (1950-51). Okay, he's out of the past, but he played a mean accordion and even did it halftime at one of his games.

Beasts of the Boards

Never forget: "Rebounds equal rings." Almost every coach in the NBA would agree with the assessment that you can't win a championship unless you rebound the basketball. You obviously can't get second shots. You can't run. You can't make the other team play your game. Some guys rebound with pure strength and size. Some do it with intelligence and positioning. Some just do it with pure effort. Every team wants a moose rebounder, but not every team has one. Here's a list of some of the players coaches dream about having on their side underneath the backboards.

1. Dennis Rodman, Chicago—He keeps the ball alive by tap, tap, tapping it and then fetching it with his endless energy. He's bizarre, but he's a great rebounder.
2. Horace Grant, Orlando—The Magic had Shaq and Penny Hardaway, but they didn't become a serious contender until they got Grant, one of the NBA's best rebounders.
3. Tyrone Hill, Cleveland—Know what "relentless" means? Watch this Cavalier play and you'll see the definition in action.
4. Dikembe Mutombo, Denver—He's such a nice guy, at least when he's not going for a rebound. When he is boarding, he doesn't like anybody.
5. Charles Oakley, New York—For years, when people talked about great, strong, hard-working rebounders, this is the one they compared everyone else to.
6. Shaquille O'Neal, Orlando—And then there are the guys who use size and strength and position all

together. Like Shaq, the NBA's strongest player.

7. Shawn Kemp, Seattle—For years, people have asked, "Is he a center or is he a forward?" Doesn't matter. He's a great rebounder.

8. Hakeem Olajuwon, Houston—You don't win two championship rings and get voted the Finals MVP two years in a row just by scoring.

9. Dale Davis, Indiana—This underrated star is a pleasure to watch if you like to see a real serious-minded rebounder at work.

10. Karl Malone, Utah—Just look at him. It's as if someone took a slab of granite and chiseled out a power forward.

11. Kevin Willis, Miami—He doesn't have the longest arms in the league, so he really must rely on positioning and effort. And he gets his double-figure rebounds on a regular basis.

12. Vin Baker, Milwaukee—In just two years, he has gone from skinny to powerful, from good to very good. Awesome and great are his next stops.

13. Patrick Ewing, New York—He has just kept working on his rebounding and over the years has become one of the league's best.

Not a Crime . . . and It Does Pay

Only in sports is it okay to steal. Baseball players steal bases. Football players steal passes. And basketball players steal the ball. It can be an art form, with different ways to do it. Some players rely on quick hands to take away the ball. Others play the passing lanes, waiting for an opponent to try to get the ball to a teammate. Either way, the best of them end up on basketball's list of Most Wanted Thieves.

1. Mookie Blaylock, Atlanta—Go ahead. Dribble the ball past him. He dares you. He double-dares you. And he gets you.
2. Gary Payton, Seattle—For the definition of "pressure defense," watch this point guard play the game. You'll discover exactly what it means.
3. Scottie Pippen, Chicago—Then, of course, there are the guys who can pick you clean off the dribble or play the passing lanes and pick off the passes.
4. Derek Harper, New York—You almost feel sorry for the rookies going against him. They're going to be victimized at least once a game; they just don't know when.
5. John Stockton, Utah—A perfect two-way player. He giveth with his assists, he taketh away with his steals. Every year.
6. Nate McMillan, Seattle—You're playing the Sonics. Gary Payton takes a rest. So just when you thought it was safe to handle the ball again, this guy shows up.
7. Hakeem Olajuwon, Houston—Big guys can steal,

too. "The Dream" can make it almost impossible for opponents to get the ball inside to their big men.

8. Robert Horry, Houston—He plays it like Pippen and Hakeem. He waits and waits, reads the pass, and then pounces. He had seven steals in one Finals game, an NBA record.

9. Anfernee (Penny) Hardaway, Orlando—It just doesn't seem fair. How can he be so good on defense when he's that good on offense?

10. Michael Jordan, Chicago—Maybe no one ever played passing lanes better than His Airness. That's just one reason why he's considered the greatest ever.

Gallery of Stars

▬ ▬ ▬

Some, like David Robinson, Hakeem Olajuwon, and John Stockton, are superstars. Others, like Jason Kidd and Grant Hill, are on the way.

You'll find them among the talented cast of players whose profiles follow.

HAKEEM OLAJUWON
"The Dream"

His nickname was fulfilled like no other NBA player in the mid-1990s.

In the 1993-94 season, Hakeem "The Dream" Olajuwon brought the city of Houston—his adopted home—its first NBA championship. He did it by averaging 27.3 points and 11.9 rebounds in the regular season, then carrying the team to playoff victories over Portland, Phoenix, Utah, and New York. The Rockets had their title. Could anything be sweeter? Yes. Another title in 1994-95, when Olajuwon was MVP of the NBA Finals once again.

It was a long way from his early days in Lagos, Nigeria, when people stared at him and kids taunted him because of his size. He was only 15 years old at the time, but had grown to a height of 6'9".

Every day, the boys in his neighborhood kept ridiculing him until he couldn't take it any longer. "I would get into fights," Olajuwon recalled. "Sometimes I would be ashamed of being so tall. I would wish I was normal height so I could be friendly with everyone."

Born January 21, 1963, in Lagos, the third child in a middle-class family of five boys and one girl, Hakeem loved sports. Since soccer was king in Nigeria, he became a goalie on his high school team. He also excelled in team handball, which in Nigeria is played on a soccer-like field with players running up and down the field and firing the ball toward a goal.

Then he started fooling around with a basketball, although he knew virtually nothing about the sport.

Nobody knew it would be the beginning of The Dream.

Recognizing Hakeem's raw athletic talents, Richard Mills, the Nigerian national basketball coach, made him the team's center, even though Mills had to teach the gangly novice how to dunk a basketball.

Then when Olajuwon turned 17, his parents, who ran a thriving cement business, encouraged him to go to college overseas. A United States State Department employee arranged for the 6'11", 190-pound teenager to visit several college campuses in the United States. When Olajuwon arrived in New York, it was cold. He wanted to go to a warmer place, so he jumped on the next plane to Houston and never left.

Olajuwon enrolled at the University of Houston as a business student in 1980. Because the "H" is silent in Hakeem, he was incorrectly given the name Akeem, but he was too polite to correct the mistake. He waited until 1991 to announce he preferred the real Arabic spelling of his name, Hakeem, which means "wise one."

When Olajuwon first joined the school's basketball team, little was expected of him. He was a foreigner and basketball was still unfamiliar to him. In fact, coach Guy

Lewis withheld him from competition his first year to teach him the fundamentals and to add muscle and weight to his thin frame. "He had no power move to the basket, he had no turnaround shot," Lewis said. "He could jump, but he didn't know when to jump or where to jump."

"We knew he'd get better," said college teammate Clyde Drexler, who would later star for Portland and rejoin him in Houston in 1994-95, "because he couldn't get any worse."

Actually, the 7-foot, 255-pounder's improvement became scary. In his sophomore year in 1982-83, he centered a run-and-gun Cougars team that won 25 straight games. Because of their high-flying, above-the-rim style, the Cougars were nicknamed "Phi Slama Jama" as Olajuwon rapidly became one of the most awesome shot-blockers in college history.

In leading Phi Slama Jama to the NCAA championship game, a 54-52 loss to North Carolina State, Olajuwon was named the tournament's MVP. He took Houston to the NCAA championship game again the next season, but the Cougars lost to Patrick Ewing and Georgetown, 84-75.

Feeling he had learned enough to compete with the best in the world, Olajuwon decided to forego his final year of college eligibility and enter the NBA Draft. The Houston Rockets made him the first overall pick in 1984 from a talent pool that also included Michael Jordan, Charles Barkley, and John Stockton.

Teamed with 7'4" Ralph Sampson to form "The Twin Towers," Olajuwon helped transform Houston into a defensive force with his shot-blocking, intimidating presence. Olajuwon worked tirelessly in the off-season to improve his offense, taking 500 shots a day, and soon became the NBA's premier all-around center. He averaged 30 points against Kareem Abdul-Jabbar in the 1986 playoffs as the Rockets eliminated the defending-champion Lakers. "In terms of raw athletic ability," marveled the Lakers' Magic Johnson, "Hakeem is the best I've ever seen."

Hakeem the Dream became a nightmare for opponents. His spin moves and fallaways were impossible to defend. Always a terror defensively, Olajuwon became the first player in NBA history to block 200 or more shots for 10 straight seasons. And he annually leads the league's centers in steals.

A devout believer in Islam, Olajuwon calls his religion "the overriding factor in my life." Yet he is grateful for his chance to play pro basketball and appreciative that he has climbed to the top of his profession. "Looking back to see how far I have grown in my career and also how the NBA has grown, I'm thankful," he said.

Hakeem is a collector of abstract art and likes to relax by painting in oils. He lives on the outskirts of Houston, but now has a fan following across the world, nowhere more than Lagos, Nigeria, where nobody is making fun of him anymore.

Year	Team	G	FG	FG Pct.	FT	FT Pct.	Reb.	Ast.	TP	Avg.
1984-85	Houston	82	677	.538	338	.613	974	111	1692	20.6
1985-86	Houston	68	625	.526	347	.645	781	137	1597	23.5
1986-87	Houston	75	677	.508	400	.702	858	220	1755	23.4
1987-88	Houston	79	712	.514	381	.695	959	163	1805	22.8
1988-89	Houston	82	790	.508	454	.696	1105	149	2034	24.8
1989-90	Houston	82	806	.501	382	.713	1149	234	1995	24.3
1990-91	Houston	56	487	.508	213	.769	770	131	1187	21.2
1991-92	Houston	70	591	.502	328	.766	845	157	1510	21.6
1992-93	Houston	82	848	.529	444	.779	1068	291	2140	26.1
1993-94	Houston	80	894	.528	388	.716	955	287	2184	27.3
1994-95	Houston	72	798	.517	406	.756	775	255	2005	27.8
	Totals	828	7905	.516	4081	.710	10239	2135	19904	24.0
	Playoff Totals	107	1208	.531	603	.715	1272	357	3023	28.3

DAVID ROBINSON
"The Admiral"

The announcement was made between games of the 1995 NBA playoffs in San Antonio: David Robinson had been named the NBA's Most Valuable Player for 1994-95.

It came as no surprise after a regular season in which the 7'1", 235-pound Spurs center had his best year since he joined the league in 1989.

"This is probably the most important award I've ever won," Robinson said at the time. "If we win a championship, that obviously will go ahead of this one."

He and his team are still missing that title. Hakeem Olajuwon and the Rockets knocked the Spurs out of the playoffs on their way to the crown. But Robinson doesn't have to make any apologies for a season that saw him finish third in the league in scoring, seventh in rebounding, and 15th in field-goal percentage and steals.

For the man they call "The Admiral," it marked a new level in a storybook career. Born August 6, 1965, in Key West, Florida, he entered the Naval Academy after playing only one year of high school basketball (Osbourne Park, Manassas, Virginia). Robinson was a 6'6", 175-pound freshman small forward at Annapolis with few basketball aspirations.

He was more academically oriented, as his Scholastic Aptitude Test score of 1,320 (out of 1,600) would indicate. When he was 14, he was taking advanced computer courses at a local college. Soon after, he assembled a 6-foot screen projection television by himself.

As a Navy freshman, Robinson averaged only 7.6 points, but then he sprouted in size, growing seven inches in two years. From then on he was unstoppable, becoming the College Player of the Year in 1987 and setting a ton of records.

He was a member of the U.S. bronze-medal team at the 1988 Olympic Games in Seoul, Korea, after he was chosen No. 1 overall by the Spurs in the 1987 NBA Draft. But he had to fulfill two years of service in the U.S. Navy before joining the pros and becoming NBA Rookie of the Year in 1989-90.

There have been many accomplishments since then: an Olympic gold medal in 1992, three times All-NBA First Team, and three times All-NBA Defensive First Team.

An officer and a gentleman, a role model for the NBA, the multitalented Robinson chose basketball over a career in the Navy. If he hadn't, he surely would have become the nation's first 7-foot admiral.

Year	Team	G	FG	FG Pct.	FT	FT Pct.	Reb.	Ast.	TP	Avg.
1989-90	San Antonio	82	690	.531	613	.732	983	164	1993	24.3
1990-91	San Antonio	82	754	.552	592	.762	1063	208	2101	25.6
1991-92	San Antonio	68	592	.551	393	.701	829	181	1578	23.2
1992-93	San Antonio	82	676	.501	561	.732	956	301	1916	23.4
1993-94	San Antonio	80	840	.507	693	.749	855	381	2383	29.8
1994-95	San Antonio	81	788	.530	656	.774	877	236	2238	27.6
Totals		475	4340	.527	3508	.744	5563	1471	12209	25.7
Playoff Totals		43	362	.483	312	.743	522	132	1037	24.1

JOHN STOCKTON
A Passing Fancy

He was at home in Utah, playing against the Denver Nuggets on February 1, 1995. A perfect setting for John Stockton, who was ready for a very special assist.

The all-time assists record was 9,921, held by Magic Johnson of the Los Angeles Lakers, and on this night, to the cheers of Jazz fans, Stockton surpassed that mark. It was the ultimate achievement—short, of course, of an NBA title—for the 6'1", 175-pound guard as he went into the book as No. 1 in the helping-hands department.

For the eighth consecutive season, Stockton led the league in assists, tying a mark set by Boston's Bob Cousy. At the end of the 1994-95 season, Stockton wound up with 10,394, a milestone in a glorious career that began with the Jazz in 1984.

"I get a lot of pleasure out of getting the ball to my teammates," Stockton said. "If I can make a good pass and help us win, it's as good as scoring a basket."

Born March 26, 1962, in Spokane, Washington, Stockton starred at Gonzaga University, where his grandfather had been an All-American halfback in the 1920s. An outstanding student, the future Jazz mainstay made the Academic All-American Second Team as a college senior.

Utah drafted him 16th for his smarts and skills in 1984, and he has been a fixture in the lineup ever since, missing only four games in 11 seasons. In 1994-95, when he was fourth in the league in steals and fifth in 3-point shooting percentage, Stockton was named to the All-NBA First Team for the second year in a row. He was also selected for the All-NBA Defensive Second Team for the fourth time and made his seventh straight All-Star Game appearance.

With teammate Karl Malone, he was co-MVP of the 1993 All-Star Game and he played on the gold-medal Dream Team in the 1992 Olympic Games in Barcelona, Spain. Stockton is also slated to be a member of the 1996 Olympic team.

He's a modest, selfless performer on his way to the Hall of Fame.

Year	Team	G	FG	FG Pct.	FT	FT Pct.	Reb.	Ast.	TP	Avg.
1984-85	Utah	82	157	.471	142	.736	105	415	458	5.6
1985-86	Utah	82	228	.489	172	.839	179	610	630	7.7
1986-87	Utah	82	231	.499	179	.782	151	670	648	7.9
1987-88	Utah	82	454	.574	272	.840	237	1128	1204	14.7
1988-89	Utah	82	497	.538	390	.863	248	1118	1400	17.1
1989-90	Utah	78	472	.514	354	.819	206	1134	1345	17.2
1990-91	Utah	82	496	.507	363	.836	237	1164	1413	17.2
1991-92	Utah	82	453	.482	308	.842	270	1126	1297	15.8
1992-93	Utah	82	437	.486	293	.798	237	987	1239	15.1
1993-94	Utah	82	458	.528	272	.805	258	1031	1236	15.1
1994-95	Utah	82	429	.542	246	.804	251	1011	1206	14.7
Totals		898	4312	.515	2991	.820	2379	10394	12076	13.4
Playoff Totals		89	455	.473	335	.819	286	980	1304	14.7

CHARLES BARKLEY
The Reign of "Sir Charles"

"Boy Gorge." "The Round Mound of Rebound." "The Leaning Tower of Pizza."

The Phoenix Suns' Charles Barkley has had many nicknames, starting with his days at Auburn University, where he was once a 300-pounder.

Now the explosive 6'5" forward tips the scales at 252 pounds and is known as "Sir Charles" because of his flamboyant dominance on and off the court. A joy to watch, incredibly quotable, and a pitchman in numerous TV commercials, he's become one of the game's leading ambassadors over the course of an 11-year career that began with the Philadelphia 76ers in 1984.

"People sometimes get mad at me because I tell the truth," Barkley once said. "But anybody who knows me, I think, likes me. I'm a spontaneous person. My momma told me a long time ago to let my emotions out, not to be repressed."

Born February 20, 1963, in Leeds, Alabama, he was raised by his mother, who cleaned houses, and his grandmother, a beautician. He was always blunt, always rambunctious, and always made people notice him.

Barkley became Auburn's fourth all-time scorer while leading the Southeastern Conference in his freshman, sophomore, and junior seasons. He decided to forego his senior year in favor of the pros and was the fifth pick, taken by the 76ers, in the 1984 NBA Draft.

In 1986-87, he became the shortest player in league history to win the rebounding title, averaging 14.6 per game. After eight years in Philadelphia and a gold-medal performance as a member of the Dream Team in the 1992 Barcelona Olympics, he was traded to the Suns for Jeff Hornacek, Andrew Lang, and Tim Perry in 1992.

Barkley became an instant smash in Phoenix, averaging 25.6 points a game and being named regular-season MVP as he paced the Suns to the 1993 NBA Finals. But Michael Jordan's Bulls ended Phoenix's bid for a championship.

Injuries have limited Barkley in recent seasons, but he keeps coming back with key contributions when it counts,like his 56-point game against Golden State in the 1994 playoffs.

He has made the All-NBA First Team five times and has played in nine straight All-Star Games. He's one of 12 players in league history to score over 19,000 points.

Barkley's fierce desire to win and his sense of humor, with which he regularly pokes fun at referees, opposing players, and teammates, make him one of the most colorful characters in sports.

Year	Team	G	FG	FG Pct.	FT	FT Pct.	Reb.	Ast.	TP	Avg.
1984-85	Philadelphia	82	427	.545	293	.733	703	155	1148	14.0
1985-86	Philadelphia	80	595	.572	396	.685	1026	312	1603	20.0
1986-87	Philadelphia	68	557	.594	429	.761	994	331	1564	23.0
1987-88	Philadelphia	80	753	.587	714	.751	951	254	2264	28.3
1988-89	Philadelphia	79	700	.579	602	.753	986	325	2037	25.8
1989-90	Philadelphia	79	706	.600	557	.749	909	307	1989	25.2
1990-91	Philadelphia	67	665	.570	475	.722	680	284	1849	27.6
1991-92	Philadelphia	75	622	.552	454	.695	830	308	1730	23.1
1992-93	Phoenix	76	716	.520	445	.765	928	385	1944	25.6
1993-94	Phoenix	65	518	.495	318	.704	727	296	1402	21.6
1994-95	Phoenix	68	554	.486	379	.748	756	276	1561	23.0
Totals		819	6813	.555	5062	.735	9490	3233	19091	23.3
Playoff Totals		95	844	.526	579	.710	1260	394	2315	24.4

JOE DUMARS
The Peerless Piston

His trademark is defense, but on the night of November 8, 1994, the Detroit Pistons' Joe Dumars ended up in the record book for a spectacular offensive performance. Playing against the Minnesota Timberwolves at the Palace of Auburn Hills, he connected for 10 3-point field goals. This equalled the all-time mark set by Brian Shaw of the Miami Heat against the Milwaukee Bucks in 1993.

The 6'3", 190-pound guard will be known less for this feat than for his contributions as a key figure with the championship Pistons in 1989 and 1990, and as a symbol of the ultimate team player.

A Piston from the beginning of an illustrious career that began in 1985, he's made the NBA All-Defensive First Team four times and has been an offensive force as well.

"Some guys take nights off in this league," said Chuck Daly, his former Detroit coach. "Not Joe. He plays all-out every game."

Born May 5, 1963, in Natchitoches, Louisiana, Dumars grew up in a football-focused family with five brothers and a sister. Brother David played in the United States Football League. But Dumars' game would be basketball. He was the all-time scoring leader at tiny McNeese State, and the Pistons chose him No. 18 in the 1985 Draft.

Dumars made the All-NBA Rookie Team in 1986 and was MVP of the 1989 NBA Finals when he averaged 27.3 points per game. He has played in five All-Star Games.

Injuries hampered him in 1993-94—although he did play for the USA Dream Team in the World Championship in Toronto—and again in 1994-95, when his scoring fell below a 20-point average for the first time in three years. But he entered the 1995-96 season, his 11th, with the optimism that has always marked his game.

Off the court, he's a giant in his commitment to the community. In 1993, Dumars began the "Joe Dumars Celebrity Tennis Classic," a charitable event that raises funds for Children's Hospital in Detroit. And in 1995 he and two business associates were the force that created the Joe Dumars Arena in the Detroit suburb of Shelby Township. It is a sports center that offers area youth a safe place to play sports and develop positive relationships.

Year	Team	G	FG	FG Pct.	FT	FT Pct.	Reb.	Ast.	TP	Avg.
1985-86	Detroit	82	287	.481	190	.798	119	390	769	9.4
1986-87	Detroit	79	369	.493	184	.748	167	352	931	11.8
1987-88	Detroit	82	453	.472	251	.815	200	387	1161	14.2
1988-89	Detroit	69	456	.505	260	.850	172	390	1186	17.2
1989-90	Detroit	75	508	.480	297	.900	212	368	1335	17.8
1990-91	Detroit	80	622	.481	371	.890	187	443	1629	20.4
1991-92	Detroit	82	587	.448	412	.867	188	375	1635	19.9
1992-93	Detroit	77	677	.466	343	.864	148	308	1809	23.5
1993-94	Detroit	69	505	.452	276	.836	151	261	1410	20.4
1994-95	Detroit	67	417	.430	277	.805	158	368	1214	18.1
Totals		762	4881	.469	2861	.844	1702	3642	13079	17.2
Playoff Totals		99	589	.466	381	.849	228	478	1591	16.1

JASON KIDD
The New Kidd on the Block

He is the next Magic Johnson. Says who? Magic Johnson.

Comments like that would seem hard to believe except that Dallas' Jason Kidd is getting a lot of rave reviews these days. "As a point guard, he has some of the greatest passing skills I have ever seen," Milwaukee Bucks coach Mike Dunleavy says. "I would put him in a class with Johnson and [John] Stockton."

And this from San Antonio Spurs general manager Gregg Popovich: "He's what every coach would fight for to have on his team because of his character qualities, as well as his ability. Competitively, he's like [Larry] Bird and Magic and Michael [Jordan]. No one competes like this guy."

Imagine what it will be like after Kidd spends some time in the NBA. He is being compared to the greatest players after just one season with the Mavericks. But what a season! He went from being the second pick in the 1994 Draft to co-Rookie of the Year with Detroit's Grant Hill and led all players, no matter what their experience, with four triple-doubles. Although it does not get much attention compared to his passing and scoring, he is also a very good defensive player.

The Mavericks were pleased, but not surprised. Born March 23, 1973, in San Francisco, Kidd was turning heads before he was even in high school. Sought by most colleges, he settled on the University of California in Berkeley, not far from his home.

He stayed there only two years before deciding to

turn pro. Now, it was the NBA teams who were all interested. Coaches and general managers saw greatness in the way Kidd could pass and dribble while also having the strength at 6'4", 212 pounds to play inside. Coincidentally, he always used to keep an old Mavericks cap in the back of his mother's car, because green was his favorite color and "I also saw myself playing in Dallas for some reason." Now the world knows he has talent as a basketball player and a psychic.

"I think that Jason Kidd is one of the most advanced and talented players to come into the league in a long time," says Charles Barkley of the Phoenix Suns. "He and Anfernee Hardaway might be the best rookies in the last 10 years . . . They're the only ones who come in with complete games. That's it. No one else."

In his first season, Kidd wound up No. 7 in the league in steals and No. 9 in assists. And soon people will be comparing other players to him.

Year	Team	G	FG	FG Pct.	FT	FT Pct.	Reb.	Ast.	TP	Avg.
1994-95	Dallas	79	330	.385	192	.698	430	607	922	11.7

DENNIS RODMAN
As the Worm Turns

He sports more tattoos that a ship full of sailors. He has dyed his hair red, blue, orange, green, and a combined red and green, which he wore one Christmas. He has his own fan club and has even dated Madonna.

No, Dennis Rodman isn't your average NBA player. Not in the least.

Nicknamed "Worm" because of his remarkable ability to worm around the basket to get rebounds, the colorful Rodman has some of the most unique skills in basketball.

Truth is, the 6'8", 210-pound Chicago Bulls forward is the NBA's preeminent defensive demon and rebounding machine. As his former Detroit Pistons teammate Isiah Thomas said, "He is as valuable defensively as [Michael] Jordan is offensively. If you would compare it to football, he is like Lawrence Taylor was."

Not only does Rodman punish teams defensively, he crashes the boards like nobody else. He has led the NBA in rebounding four straight years (1992-93-94-95), a feat only accomplished by Wilt Chamberlain and Moses Malone.

Born May 13, 1961, in Trenton, New Jersey, Rodman grew up in Dallas but never played high school ball. Because of that he wasn't recruited by major college powers. So he played at Cooke County Junior College in Texas before moving on to Southeastern Oklahoma, where he led the NAIA in rebounding in 1985.

Not long after the Pistons selected him with the 27th pick (second round) in the 1986 Draft, a star was born. With his great leaping ability and boundless drive, Rodman helped Detroit win back-to-back NBA championships in 1989 and 1990. He was named the league's Defensive Player of the Year in 1990 and 1991 and has been NBA All-Defensive First Team for six years.

Traded to San Antonio in 1993 for Sean Elliott and David Wood, and now with the Bulls, Rodman certainly created waves with his eccentric look and rebellious image. But his immense on-court value has never been lost on his appreciative teammates. "Dennis taught me more about how to win—how to play winning basketball—than any other player I've ever played with," said Spurs superstar center David Robinson. "His spirit and hustle are amazing."

Year	Team	G	FG	FG Pct.	FT	FT Pct.	Reb.	Ast.	TP	Avg.
1986-87	Detroit	77	213	.545	74	.587	332	56	500	6.5
1987-88	Detroit	82	398	.561	152	.535	715	110	953	11.6
1988-89	Detroit	82	316	.595	97	.626	772	99	735	9.0
1989-90	Detroit	82	288	.581	142	.654	792	72	719	8.8
1990-91	Detroit	82	276	.493	111	.631	1026	85	669	8.2
1991-92	Detroit	82	342	.539	84	.600	1530	191	800	9.8
1992-93	Detroit	62	183	.427	87	.534	1132	102	468	7.5
1993-94	San Antonio	79	156	.534	53	.520	1367	184	370	4.7
1994-95	San Antonio	49	137	.571	75	.676	823	97	349	7.1
	Totals	677	2309	.539	875	.594	8489	996	5563	8.2
	Playoff Totals	111	323	.527	117	.511	1021	100	765	6.9

KARL MALONE
A Sure Thing

There's an old saying that the only sure things in life are death and taxes. But in the NBA, there's another sure thing: Karl Malone will go out, play every game, and get his usual 26 points and 11 rebounds.

Since joining the Utah Jazz in 1985, "The Mailman" has played in 816 out of a possible 820 games. Entering the 1995-96 season, his 26.0 scoring average was seventh-best in NBA history, and he ranked No. 1 in the Jazz record books in points and rebounds.

What's the key to Malone's success? Raw, brute strength.

"Karl is so big and strong, once he gets the ball inside you can put two points in the book," said Utah coach Jerry Sloan. "The great thing is how hard he's worked and how far he's come."

The 6'9", 256-pound forward was born July 24, 1963, in Summerfield, Louisiana, the second of nine children. He starred at Louisiana Tech, becoming the school's third all-time leading scorer. It was during his stay there that a sportswriter tagged him with his "Mailman" nickname because "he always delivers."

Malone left school after his junior year and was selected by the Jazz with the 13th pick in the 1985 NBA Draft. He started slowly, averaging only 14.9 points his rookie season, but still was named to the NBA All-Rookie Team.

Since that rookie season, Malone has never averaged below 21 points per game, with a best of 31.0 in 1989-90. When his average dropped for four consecutive seasons after that, it was thought that the physical, grinding style Malone employs was starting to wear him down.

But that wasn't the case in 1994-95 as he bounced back with a 26.7 average, the highest of any non-center in the league, and became the 19th player in NBA history to accumulate 20,000 points. Of those 19 players, only Wilt Chamberlain, Michael Jordan, Oscar Robertson, and Kareem Abdul-Jabbar cracked the 20,000 plateau in fewer games than Malone.

He played in the 1992 Olympic Games in Barcelona and took home a gold medal, as did Jazz teammate John Stockton. (Malone was also named to the 1996 Olympic team.) During the off-season, he gets in his customized 16-wheel truck and transports food and equipment throughout Utah and the surrounding area. So even when he's not on the court, "The Mailman" continues to deliver.

Year	Team	G	FG	FG Pct.	FT	FT Pct.	Reb.	Ast.	TP	Avg.
1985-86	Utah	81	504	.496	195	.481	718	236	1203	14.9
1986-87	Utah	82	728	.512	323	.598	855	158	1779	21.7
1987-88	Utah	82	858	.520	552	.700	986	199	2268	27.7
1988-89	Utah	80	809	.519	703	.766	853	219	2326	29.1
1989-90	Utah	82	914	.562	696	.762	911	226	2540	31.0
1990-91	Utah	82	847	.527	684	.770	967	270	2382	29.0
1991-92	Utah	81	798	.526	673	.778	909	241	2272	28.0
1992-93	Utah	82	797	.552	619	.740	919	308	2217	27.0
1993-94	Utah	82	772	.497	511	.694	940	328	2063	25.2
1994-95	Utah	82	830	.536	516	.742	871	285	2187	26.7
Totals		816	7857	.526	5472	.721	8929	2470	21237	26.0
Playoff Totals		79	770	.476	627	.757	925	196	2169	27.5

REGGIE MILLER
Beating the Clock

The game was in the bag. The Knicks led the Pacers by six points with 16 seconds left. It was Game 1 of the 1995 Eastern Conference semifinals and the Madison Square Garden crowd was already rejoicing. Even the Knicks players on the bench were whooping it up.

But then came Miller Time.

In one of the most astounding one-man shows in NBA history, Reggie Miller, Indiana's electrifying 6'7", 185-pound guard literally stole the game away from the Knicks. He drilled a 3-pointer, snatched an inbounds pass, knocked down another three, then hit two pressure free throws—all in under 16 seconds!

Doing the incredible is nothing new to Miller. Only one year earlier, he sank the Knicks in a playoff game with a mind-boggling 25-point fourth quarter, including five 3-pointers, sending Garden fans into a state of shock.

Despite his flashy, legend-making playoff moments, national recognition has come late to Miller. This is partly because of his earlier inconsistency, partly because he plays in Indianapolis, a smaller-market city, and partly because of his older sister, Cheryl, a former U.S. Olympian who was inducted into the Basketball Hall of Fame in 1994.

"Overcoming my sister's shadow," Reggie admitted, "has been the biggest obstacle of my life."

Born August 24, 1965, in Riverside, California, Miller developed his shooting skills as a kid, thanks to some fierce one-on-one games with Cheryl. He attended UCLA, where he was among the nation's top scorers as a junior and senior. After the Pacers made him the 11th selection of the 1987 Draft, Miller shot his way through the Indiana record books, becoming the franchise's all-time scorer.

He is one of the league's most lethal 3-point threats. With his lightning-quick release and feisty competitive spirit, Miller became the first player in NBA history to make 100 or more 3-pointers in six straight seasons. He has 1,035 career 3-pointers, second only to Dale Ellis' 1,119. He'll be a member of the U.S. team in the 1996 Olympic Games at Atlanta.

Bold, brazen, and brilliant, Miller is now one of the league's biggest attractions. After all, the finger-waving, jump-shooting superstar is able to turn basketball games upside-down in a matter of seconds.

Year	Team	G	FG	FG Pct.	FT	FT Pct.	Reb.	Ast.	TP	Avg.
1987-88	Indiana	82	306	.488	149	.801	190	132	822	10.0
1988-89	Indiana	74	398	.479	287	.844	292	227	1181	16.0
1989-90	Indiana	82	661	.514	544	.868	295	311	2016	24.6
1990-91	Indiana	82	596	.512	551	.918	281	331	1855	22.6
1991-92	Indiana	82	562	.501	442	.858	318	314	1695	20.7
1992-93	Indiana	82	571	.479	427	.880	258	262	1736	21.2
1993-94	Indiana	79	524	.503	403	.908	212	248	1574	19.9
1994-95	Indiana	81	505	.462	383	.897	210	242	1588	19.6
Totals		644	4123	.493	3186	.879	2056	2067	12467	19.4
Playoff Totals		48	378	.483	309	.861	156	127	1182	24.6

SHAWN KEMP
A Sonic Boom

It intimidates opponents. It entertains fans. And it draws admiration from teammates. "It" is one of Shawn Kemp's arm-swirling, all-out, gravity-defying slam dunks.

"I've never seen anyone jump as high as Kemp," marveled Shaquille O'Neal, no stranger to dynamic dunks himself. "He really gets airborne."

But perhaps Kemp's most remarkable move is that he is one of only a handful of players ever to go right from high school to the NBA. His skills are still developing. But the electricity and power the Seattle Sonics' 6'10", 245-pound forward brings to the court have already made him one of the NBA's most fun players to watch.

Born November 26, 1969, in Elkhart, Indiana, Kemp has always motivated himself to play better. Growing up fatherless, he was motivated to work harder as a boy. Being denied the prestigious "Mr.

Basketball" honor in high school in Indiana only further fueled his intensity.

At age 19, Kemp was selected by the Sonics as the 17th selection in the 1989 Draft. He quickly showed the potential of a superstar as his incredible moves, shot-blocking, rebounding, and scoring began turning heads. In six years in the NBA, Kemp has already passed Jack Sikma as Seattle's all-time shot-blocker and is second on the club's all-time rebounding list.

Kemp has been in the All-Star Game the last three seasons (twice as a starter), and excelled as a member of USA Dream Team in the 1994 World Championship in Toronto.

How popular is Kemp? When there was talk he would be traded by the Sonics in the summer of 1994, Seattle fans flooded the radio shows and the team's offices with calls demanding that the deal not go through. Seattle management obviously heeded the calls. The deal was halted. With good reason.

Year	Team	G	FG	FG Pct.	FT	FT Pct.	Reb.	Ast.	TP	Avg.
1989-90	Seattle	81	203	.479	117	.736	346	26	525	6.5
1990-91	Seattle	81	462	.508	288	.661	679	144	1214	15.0
1991-92	Seattle	64	362	.504	270	.748	665	86	994	15.5
1992-93	Seattle	78	515	.492	358	.712	833	155	1388	17.8
1993-94	Seattle	79	533	.538	364	.741	851	207	1431	18.1
1994-95	Seattle	82	545	.547	438	.749	893	149	1530	18.7
	Totals	465	2620	.515	1835	.724	4267	767	7082	15.2
	Playoff Totals	42	239	.478	230	.782	433	87	709	16.9

GRANT HILL
King of the Hill

Grant Hill was born into a world of success. His father Calvin attended Yale and became a standout running back in the National Football League and the World Football League from 1969-81. His mother Janet roomed with Hillary Rodham Clinton at Wellesley and is now a lawyer in the Washington, D.C., area.

Imagine being a kid having to live up to those credentials. But the young Hill did it, and more.

During his formative years, Grant looked up to tennis immortal Arthur Ashe and basketball's Julius Erving, role models who would serve him well later on. He went to high school in Reston, Virginia, and then chose to attend Duke, a university equally respected for basketball and academics. Once there, he played on two NCAA championship teams and won numerous individual awards, including being named the best defensive player in the country as a junior while everyone was talking about his offensive brilliance.

Finally, he was starting to break out and make a name for himself. In college, he was a talent, but still relegated to a supporting role behind the stars of the moment, of which Duke had many. Now it was Hill's turn.

It started in his junior season, when he averaged 18 points a game and was named a second team All-American. Not only that, but pro scouts took notice of the 6'8", 225-pounder who was able to handle the ball well enough to play some point guard.

After one more season, the pros had their chance.

Hill went third overall to the Detroit Pistons in the 1994 Draft and became an immediate hit because his personality matched his skills. Like Ashe and Erving, he was a pleasure to be around, treated everyone with respect and, in general, seemed far more mature than someone who had just turned 22 the week training camp started. Companies like Coke, Fila, and General Motors quickly signed him to commercial deals.

That popularity with fans transcended to the court, where he was voted a starter in the All-Star Game despite being a first-year player. He wound up being named co-Rookie of the Year with Dallas' Jason Kidd. And such was his appeal, he made not one, but two appearances on "The Late Show with David Letterman."

Year	Team	G	FG	FG Pct.	FT	FT Pct.	Reb.	Ast.	TP	Avg.
1994-95	Detroit	70	508	.477	374	.732	445	353	1394	19.9

NICK VAN EXEL
A Joy to Watch

Growing up, his goals were modest. Nick Van Exel, then in high school basketball in Kenosha, Wisconsin, wanted to be good enough to play at a college that would appear on TV. He wanted his friends and family to see him play.

Fast forward about six or seven years. Now it's impossible not to see him. There he is, leading the Los Angeles Lakers past the Seattle Sonics in the first round of the 1995 playoffs. And, look, now he's hitting miraculous shots against the San Antonio Spurs in the next round.

These are not fleeting glimpses, either. The 6'1", 170-pound Van Exel is the leader of the Lakers and one of the best young players in the league after just two pro seasons. Those same friends and family have noticed, and so have a lot of other people.

"When they talk about young players who are going to be stars," says Charles Barkley of the Phoenix Suns, "they'd better mention his name more often."

It wasn't always like this, of course. Born November 27, 1971, in Kenosha, Van Exel was the top scorer in all of Wisconsin as a high-school senior, but few colleges showed any serious interest. So he enrolled at Trinity Valley Community College in Texas. But that was only a short stop on the way to the University of Cincinnati, where, indeed, he appeared on TV as one of the Bearcats' all-time great performers. Among other feats, he established a single-game school record of eight 3-pointers and led Cincinnati to an 18–2 mark and an NCAA Final Four berth in 1991-92.

Van Exel was considered a prime NBA prospect, but he slid all the way down to the second round as the 37th choice in the 1993 Draft. It was the surprise of the day. It was also the Lakers' good fortune.

He took over as their starting point guard almost instantly, then played in the first-ever Rookie All-Star Game and ultimately made the All-Rookie Second Team.

In his second season, 1994-95, Van Exel set team single-season records for 3-pointers made (183) and attempted (511), and gained the respect of teammates and the adulation of fans.

They loved his quickness, intelligence, and enthusiastic style of play that came to embody the entire club. The Lakers were fun to watch, and Van Exel was the most fun.

Year	Team	G	FG	FG Pct.	FT	FT Pct.	Reb.	Ast.	TP	Avg.
1993-94	L.A. Lakers	81	413	.394	150	.781	238	466	1099	13.6
1994-95	L.A. Lakers	80	465	.420	235	.783	223	660	1348	16.9
	Totals	161	878	.407	385	.783	461	1126	2447	15.2
Playoff Totals		10	67	.414	45	.763	38	73	200	20.0

MOOKIE BLAYLOCK
Man of Steal

Daron Oshay Blaylock—better known as Mookie—was born March 20, 1967, in Garland, Texas, starred there in high school, played college ball at a prominent school, and was a first-round draft pick in 1989. But it wasn't until several years later that people realized how good he was.

Maybe it was the passage of time. Maybe it was the good fortune of hooking up with a coach like Lenny Wilkens in Atlanta. Or maybe it was a combination of things. Whatever the reason, Mookie Blaylock has blossomed into an NBA star.

The Hawks traded another guard, Rumeal Robinson, to the New Jersey Nets to get him. That was November 3, 1992, and it didn't take long for the deal to be considered a steal.

While Robinson drifted into obscurity, the 6'1", 185-pound Blaylock, after a so-so season in 1992-93, took off when Wilkens took over as the Hawks' coach. Now partnered with a sideline boss who emphasized defense, one of his strong points, Blaylock made the NBA All-Defensive First Team in 1993-94, and again in 1994-95. This honor carries special meaning because it is determined by the voting of opposing coaches.

Defense had always been a prominent part of his game. While starring at Oklahoma, Blaylock set the NCAA Division I record for steals in a season with 150 in 1987-88. He also set the mark for swipes in a game at 13—and did that twice.

When it was time for the NBA Draft in 1989, the Nets took him 12th. After three seasons, they traded him to Atlanta, where his career took off.

On March 22, 1995, Blaylock became the fourth-fastest player in NBA history to get 1,000 steals. In his three seasons in Atlanta, he established the three highest steal totals in franchise history, topped by his 212 in 1993-94. He finished third in the league in that category that season and moved up to second in 1994-95.

He is not, however, one-dimensional. Blaylock has also set Hawks records for 3-point shots attempted and made in a season. He has never been known as an accurate shooter, but in 1994-95, when Wilkens needed him to pick up some of the scoring slack, Blaylock's scoring average rose to 17.2, easily a career best.

There's certainly no need to wonder any more about recognition for this ball-stealing star.

Year	Team	G	FG	FG Pct.	FT	FT Pct.	Reb.	Ast.	TP	Avg.
1989-90	New Jersey	50	212	.371	63	.778	140	210	505	10.1
1990-91	New Jersey	72	432	.416	139	.790	249	441	1017	14.1
1991-92	New Jersey	72	429	.432	126	.712	269	492	996	13.8
1992-93	Atlanta	80	414	.429	123	.728	280	671	1069	13.4
1993-94	Atlanta	81	444	.411	116	.730	424	789	1118	13.8
1994-95	Atlanta	80	509	.425	156	.729	393	616	1373	17.2
	Totals	435	2440	.418	723	.741	1755	3219	6078	14.0
	Playoff Totals	21	92	.341	40	.784	97	159	262	12.5

PATRICK EWING
Center of Tenacity

He grew up on the island of Jamaica, and moved to Cambridge, Massachusetts, when he was 11 years old. Tall, yet often clumsy and awkward, Patrick Ewing tried his hand at basketball—and pursued it with a purposefulness that would mark his entire basketball career.

"Patrick was a hard worker," said Mike Jarvis, Ewing's coach at Cambridge Rindge & Latin High School, "and if he didn't know something, he'd ask you a thousand times until he got it right."

That work ethic, combined with wondrous physical skills, helped turn Ewing into one of the preeminent centers in basketball history.

Born August 5, 1962, in Kingston, Jamaica, Ewing quickly grew accustomed to winning. He led his high-school team to the state championship, and carried Georgetown to three NCAA championship games, winning over Hakeem Olajuwon and the University of Houston in 1984.

Renowned for his shot-blocking and all-out effort, Ewing won a gold medal as a member of the 1984 U.S. Olympic team. He would win more gold as a member of the Dream Team in the 1992 Olympics.

Upon graduating from Georgetown in 1985 with a degree in Art History, Ewing was selected by the New York Knicks as the No. 1 pick in the first-ever Draft Lottery. After winning Rookie-of-the-Year honors, he has become a perennial All-Star, never averaging less than 20 points a year in his 10 NBA seasons.

Although the 7-foot, 240-pounder has always been a defensive-minded player, he is also considered the best jump-shooting center ever. The Knicks have yet to win an NBA title with Ewing, but he has become the mainstay of the franchise, the hub around which the team revolves. And with his trademark determination, he remains fiercely focused on getting that elusive ring.

"Patrick has been a special player," said former Knicks great Willis Reed, "and nobody deserves it more than he."

Year	Team	G	FG	FG Pct.	FT	FT Pct.	Reb.	Ast.	TP	Avg.
1985-86	New York	50	386	.474	226	.739	451	102	998	20.0
1986-87	New York	63	530	.503	296	.713	555	104	1356	21.5
1987-88	New York	82	656	.555	341	.716	676	125	1653	20.2
1988-89	New York	80	727	.567	361	.746	740	188	1815	22.7
1989-90	New York	82	922	.551	502	.775	893	182	2347	28.6
1990-91	New York	81	845	.514	464	.745	905	244	2154	26.6
1991-92	New York	82	796	.522	377	.738	921	156	1970	24.0
1992-93	New York	81	779	.503	400	.719	980	151	1959	24.2
1993-94	New York	79	745	.496	445	.765	885	179	1939	24.5
1994-95	New York	79	730	.503	420	.750	876	212	1886	23.9
Totals		759	7116	.520	3832	.742	7873	1643	18077	23.8
Playoff Totals		89	794	.477	413	.741	972	222	2008	22.6

GLEN RICE
A Hot Hornet

He can't palm a basketball, something most NBA players can do. But he sure can shoot it.

On April 15, 1995, Glen Rice hit for 56 points for the Miami Heat against the Orlando Magic, one giant feat for anyone, let alone a big guy with little hands.

"If I could palm a basketball, I could do a lot more when I go to the basket," said the 6'8", 200-pound guard-forward, who's now with the Charlotte Hornets. (Rice joined the Hornets as a result of the trade that brought Alonzo Mourning to the Heat prior to the 1995–96 season.)

In 1994-95, Rice tied his career high with a 23.2 scoring average, ninth-best in the league. He was the Heat's leading scorer for four years and the team's top 3-point shooter. He has made at least 130 treys for four straight years (185 in 1994-95).

"Glen has a star's mentality and charisma," said former Heat coach Kevin Loughery. "He can shoot the three. And that's what fans are looking for. They want to see players dunk, shoot the 3-point shot, block shots, or make the great pass. Glen can do all of that."

Born May 28, 1967, in Flint, Michigan, he was named "Mr. Basketball" in the state as a schoolboy. He led Michigan to the NCAA title in 1989. In the championship game against Seton Hall, Rice scored 31 points and grabbed 11 rebounds. For his accomplishments, he won the Jesse Owens award that goes to the top athlete in the Big Ten Conference in any sport. When he left the Wolverines, he was the Big Ten's all-time leading scorer.

"You can never let Glen get free," said Cleveland Cavs coach Mike Fratello. "He'll kill you with his long-range shots. He's the one guy we always pay attention to."

Little hands and all.

Year	Team	G	FG	FG Pct.	FT	FT Pct.	Reb.	Ast.	TP	Avg.
1989-90	Miami	77	470	.439	91	.734	352	138	1048	13.6
1990-91	Miami	77	550	.461	171	.818	381	189	1342	17.4
1991-92	Miami	79	672	.469	266	.836	394	184	1765	22.3
1992-93	Miami	82	582	.440	242	.820	424	180	1554	19.0
1993-94	Miami	81	663	.467	250	.880	434	184	1708	21.1
1994-95	Miami	82	667	.475	312	.855	378	192	1831	22.3
Totals		478	3604	.459	1332	.835	2363	1067	9248	19.3
Playoff Totals		8	50	.379	12	.800	46	15	122	15.3

ROD STRICKLAND
A Point Well Made

He grew up perfecting his game in New York City, playing against the likes of Mark Jackson, Kenny Smith, and Pearl Washington. Years later, they would all make the NBA.

That was then. This is now: Rod Strickland of the Portland Trail Blazers isn't part of the pack anymore, having emerged as the best of that group and, even more impressively, one of the best point guards in the game. He is not considered on the same level as John Stockton, Anfernee Hardaway, or Gary Payton, but few little men are feared as much.

Strickland—a 6'3", 185-pounder—is blessed with quickness that makes it nearly impossible for an opposing defender to stay with him. In fact, many have argued, no one is better at getting by his man and then driving down the lane, where he can then drop the ball off to a waiting teammate or go for the short jumper or layup. That's a main reason he finished fourth in the NBA in assists in 1994-95 and why, after just three seasons, he's already No. 5 on the Trail Blazers' all-time assist list.

To many, he never should have been in Portland in the first place. His future was supposed to be in his hometown. Strickland was born July 11, 1966, in the Bronx. After he played for DePaul University he was drafted 19th overall by the Knicks in 1989. But he lasted only $1\frac{1}{2}$ seasons in New York, at which point he was traded to San Antonio.

Strickland spent the rest of that season and two more with the Spurs, always averaging about 14 points a game. At the same time, though, his new team questioned his maturity and commitment, so they decided not to re-sign him as a free agent in the summer of 1992. That turned out to be a huge mistake.

While San Antonio spent years searching for a reliable point guard, Strickland joined Portland and flourished. Teammates there voted him the Trail Blazers' Most Valuable Player two seasons in a row, and he received an equally noteworthy tribute from Dallas Mavericks coach Dick Motta: "He makes a lot of their good people great people."

Year	Team	G	FG	FG Pct.	FT	FT Pct.	Reb.	Ast.	TP	Avg.
1988-89	New York	81	265	.467	172	.745	160	319	721	8.9
1989-90	N.Y.–S.A.	82	343	.454	174	.626	259	468	868	10.6
1990-91	San Antonio	58	314	.482	161	.763	219	463	800	13.8
1991-92	San Antonio	57	300	.455	182	.687	265	491	787	13.8
1992-93	Portland	78	396	.485	273	.717	337	559	1069	13.7
1993-94	Portland	82	528	.483	353	.749	370	740	1411	17.2
1994-95	Portland	64	441	.466	283	.745	317	562	1211	18.9
	Totals	502	2587	.471	1598	.721	1927	3602	6867	13.7
	Playoff Totals	36	203	.447	92	.708	148	304	501	13.9

CLIFFORD ROBINSON
From Football to the Hoop

He grew up thinking football—dreaming of one day playing quarterback for his home-team Buffalo Bills. But Clifford Robinson, signal-caller for the junior varsity team at Riverside High School, soon had a problem—a growth problem.

He shot up in height and was deemed too tall to be a quarterback. So he turned his sights on the basketball hoop and became one of the top schoolboy prospects in the nation. Robinson enrolled at the University of Connecticut, where the 6'10", 225-pounder led the Huskies in scoring for three seasons and paced the team in steals and blocked shots as a senior.

A sure thing in the pros? Nothing is guaranteed in the NBA. Robinson didn't get taken until the second round (No. 36) in the 1989 NBA Draft and played mostly in reserve roles. "I just kept working hard and believing in myself," he said.

It all paid off in 1992-93, when the NBA named him

Sixth Man of the Year. The following season, Robinson, normally a forward, started 61 games at center and his 20.1 points per game made him No. 1 on the team and No. 15 in the league. And he played in his first All-Star Game.

In 1994-95 he soared in the 3-point department with 142 (he'd only had a total of 51 3-pointers in his previous five seasons) and his points-per-game average was 21.3, his best ever.

"Few guys Cliff's size can get up and down the floor like he can," said former teammate Clyde Drexler. "Cliff's got a world of athletic ability."

He is also a model of endurance. Until he sprained an ankle in 1995, he had a streak of 461 consecutive appearances. In six seasons, he has played in all but seven games.

Robinson was born December 16, 1966, in Albion, New York. He has a sister, Alisa, who played basketball at Canisius College in Buffalo.

The Robinson family roots for the Trail Blazers, but they regret that they can't cheer Cliff as a giant quarterback for the Buffalo Bills.

Year	Team	G	FG	FG Pct.	FT	FT Pct.	Reb.	Ast.	TP	Avg.
1989-90	Portland	82	298	.397	138	.550	308	72	746	9.1
1990-91	Portland	82	373	.463	205	.653	349	151	957	11.7
1991-92	Portland	82	398	.466	219	.664	416	137	1016	12.4
1992-93	Portland	82	632	.473	287	.690	542	182	1570	19.1
1993-94	Portland	82	641	.457	352	.765	550	159	1647	20.1
1994-95	Portland	75	597	.452	265	.694	423	198	1601	21.3
	Totals	485	2939	.454	1466	.681	2588	899	7537	15.5
	Playoff Totals	69	269	.420	136	.557	299	108	682	9.9

DIKEMBE MUTOMBO
Sky High in Denver

The toughest job belongs to opposing players. The second-toughest belongs to the public-address announcer at the home games who introduces the Nuggets' starting center by using his entire name.

Dikembe Mutombo Mpolondo Mukamba Jean Jacque Wamutombo.

The rest of the NBA knows him as simply Dikembe Mutombo. Or, on his really good days, "Trouble". Mutombo is 7'2", 245 pounds, and one of the most dominating defensive players in the game. How dominating? He has led the NBA in blocked shots each of the last two seasons, and in 1994-95 also finished second in rebounding. The three years before that, he finished sixth, third, and third, and his career average is an impressive 12.5 rebounds a game.

The only thing that rivals his success on the court is his intellectual achievements. The Zaire native—born June 25, 1966, in Kinshasa—speaks English, French, Portuguese, Spanish, and five African dialects. While attending Georgetown, he worked as an intern on Capitol Hill and then as a computer and translation specialist at the World Bank. After earning a degree from Georgetown in linguistics and diplomacy, he still took some postgraduate classes following his rookie season in the spring of 1992.

In short, it's been quite a road since Mutombo left Africa to come to college in the United States in 1987. At Georgetown, he was named the Big East Conference Defensive Player of the Year as a senior and the season before shared the honor with teammate Alonzo Mourning. By the time he left the Hoyas, Mutombo was second only to Patrick Ewing on the school's all-time list for blocked shots.

"I have a big heart," Mutombo once said. "I've always had a big heart. I got my big heart from my family. They are really strong. And when you have a big heart, you can do what you want to do."

The Nuggets picked him fourth overall in the 1991 Draft, and he immediately became a star, finishing No. 2 in balloting to Larry Johnson for Rookie of the Year. Within three seasons, he was the franchise leader in blocked shots.

Meanwhile, a player who once appeared clumsy when he had the ball is improving his offense all the time, proving the only thing more scary than Mutombo on defense is Mutombo at both ends of the court. That's trouble by any name.

Year	Team	G	FG	FG Pct.	FT	FT Pct.	Reb.	Ast.	TP	Avg.
1991-92	Denver	71	428	.493	321	.642	870	156	1177	16.6
1992-93	Denver	82	398	.510	335	.681	1070	147	1131	13.8
1993-94	Denver	82	365	.569	256	.583	971	127	986	12.0
1994-95	Denver	82	349	.556	248	.654	1029	113	946	11.5
	Totals	317	1540	.527	1160	.641	3940	543	4240	13.5
	Playoff Totals	15	56	.475	65	.607	163	22	177	11.8

DANA BARROS
Little Man Becomes a Big Shot

No one ever doubted he could play pro basketball, which is why the Seattle Sonics drafted Dana Barros in the first round of the 1989 Draft, the Philadelphia 76ers traded for him in the fall of 1993, and the Boston Celtics acquired him in 1995.

The main question has always been in which position to play him.

Barros has the size of a point guard (5'11", 163 pounds) but a game that is better suited for off-guard because he shoots so well. That was the reason he had trouble breaking through in the crowded backcourt in Seattle. Even in 1991-92, when the former Boston College star led the NBA in 3-point percentage, he still averaged only 17.7 minutes a game.

Finally, after one more season with the Sonics, giving him four in all, Barros was traded to Charlotte, but only for a couple of days. The ultimate destination, on September 3, 1993, was Philadelphia.

Was it ever the ultimate! With a former talented point guard, John Lucas, as his new coach with the 76ers, Barros played his usual role as the primary ball-handler, but was also given the freedom to shoot a lot.

The result was a breakout season in 1994-95. He played in the All-Star Game in February, only the seventh person smaller than six feet to be so honored. And a few months later, his great strides were recognized when he was named the league's Most Improved Player after averaging 20.6 points. Now he's back in his hometown.

Born April 13, 1967, in Boston, Barros progressed so well during his early years he probably never thought he would have to win such an award to become a star in the pros. He was a standout wide receiver and defensive back in football during high school in Westwood, Massachusetts, and went on to become a standout guard in basketball at Boston College. Once there, he became the first player to lead the Big East Conference in scoring two years in a row.

Seattle took him 16th overall in the 1989 Draft, just before the Sonics also drafted Shawn Kemp. The chance Barros never got in Seattle became the opportunity he would not miss in Philadelphia.

Year	Team	G	FG	FG Pct.	FT	FT Pct.	Reb.	Ast.	TP	Avg.
1989-90	Seattle	81	299	.405	89	.809	132	205	782	9.7
1990-91	Seattle	66	154	.495	78	.918	71	111	418	6.3
1991-92	Seattle	75	238	.483	60	.759	81	125	619	8.3
1992-93	Seattle	69	214	.451	49	.831	107	151	541	7.8
1993-94	Philadelphia	81	412	.469	116	.800	196	424	1075	13.3
1994-95	Philadelphia	82	571	.490	347	.899	274	619	1686	20.6
	Totals	454	1888	.465	739	.855	861	1635	5121	11.3
	Playoff Totals	26	52	.520	9	.750	23	25	130	5.0

JAMAL MASHBURN
A Monster "Mash"

Too heavy, some people said. Not big enough to play forward, others claimed. Jamal Mashburn heard the comments during his junior year at the University of Kentucky, but he wouldn't let the criticism bother him. Instead, he made himself eligible for the 1993 NBA Draft, and the rest, as they say, is history.

Mashburn, a 6'8", 240-pounder, was taken fourth in the first round by the Dallas Mavericks and immediately made himself at home among the league's elite forwards. "He's the most well-rounded rookie I've seen this year," Detroit's Joe Dumars said during the 1993-94 season in which "Mash" averaged 19.2 points and earned a spot on the NBA All-Rookie team.

"He's hard to play against because he's so versatile," said Phoenix Suns forward Charles Barkley, who came into the league hearing many of the same criticisms Mashburn heard. "He has the game of a forward but the skills of a guard. He can beat you in a lot of different ways."

Mashburn perfected his skills by working on his game as a youngster growing up in New York City, where he was born November 29, 1972. He played basketball virtually year-round, leading Cardinal Hayes High School to its first city championship in 50 years, then spending the summer playing in the famed Rucker League, which had produced stars like Julius Erving and Connie Hawkins.

After high school, Jamal became an All-American at Kentucky, leading the Wildcats to two consecutive Southeastern Conference titles and the NCAA Final Four in 1993. Before his rookie season he went back to Lexington, Kentucky, and donated $500,000 as part of a scholarship fund for eighth-grade students. "I see this as my chance to give something back to the people who have helped me and to help those students who may not otherwise get a chance," he explained.

In just two seasons in the NBA, Mashburn has become a symbol of the young, strong Mavericks. In 1994-95, he finished fifth in the league in scoring (24.1) and his 1,926 points were the most by a Maverick in seven years. There were no critics left.

Year	Team	G	FG	FG Pct.	FT	FT Pct.	Reb.	Ast.	TP	Avg.
1993-94	Dallas	79	561	.406	306	.699	353	266	1513	19.2
1994-95	Dallas	80	683	.436	447	.739	331	298	1926	24.1
	Totals	159	1244	.422	753	.722	684	564	3439	21.6

LATRELL SPREWELL
Shooting Spree

How impressive was Golden State Warriors guard Latrell Sprewell in his first three seasons in the NBA? Well, let's ask Pacers All-Star guard Reggie Miller.

"Next to Michael Jordan, he's got to be the quickest two-guard with the ball that I've ever played against," said Miller. "He can shoot, run the floor, jump, and he doesn't get tired."

That's high praise for a player who wasn't immediately accepted at Golden State. Warriors fans thought the team needed a center in 1992 and reacted angrily when the team selected the 6'5", 195-pound Sprewell with the 24th pick in the Draft. But "Spree" quickly turned those jeers into cheers once the season started. He finished the year fifth among all NBA rookies in scoring (15.4) and first in assists (295).

"He was the steal of the draft," said former Kings general manager Jerry Reynolds.

Sprewell was even better his second season, finishing 11th in the league with a 21.0 scoring average and leading all NBA guards in blocked shots. In 1994-95, he averaged 20.6 points and was named a starter in the All-Star Game for the first time.

"I didn't know who he was at first," Kings guard Mitch Richmond admitted. "Now everybody knows who he is."

Born September 8, 1970, in Milwaukee, Wisconsin, Sprewell didn't play high school ball until his senior year at Washington High, where he also competed in the long jump and triple jump. He went on to play two years at Three Rivers Community College in Poplar Bluff, Missouri, before heading for Alabama. Despite being overshadowed there by teammates Robert Horry (now with Houston) and James Robinson (now with Portland), Sprewell averaged 17.8 points his senior season and was named to the All-Southeastern Conference first team, along with Horry and a Louisiana State center named Shaquille O'Neal.

People might have wondered who Sprewell was then, but no one is wondering now.

"When I'm not in the game, I sit and have fun watching him," former teammate Billy Owens said. "There's hardly anything he can't do. I've often thought he could be the next Michael Jordan."

Year	Team	G	FG	FG Pct.	FT	FT Pct.	Reb.	Ast.	TP	Avg.
1992-93	Golden State	77	449	.464	211	.746	271	295	1182	15.4
1993-94	Golden State	82	613	.433	353	.774	401	385	1720	21.0
1994-95	Golden State	69	490	.418	350	.781	256	279	1420	20.6
	Totals	228	1552	.436	914	.770	928	959	4322	19.0
Playoff Totals........................		3	26	.433	8	.667	9	21	68	22.7

GLENN ROBINSON
"Big Dog"

At first glance, Glenn Robinson of the Milwaukee Bucks looks like a basketball natural. That's how good he is. But take another look at this 6'7", 225-pounder. This is the same guy who refused to try out for his seventh-grade team because he thought he was not good enough. That's right. He earned the honor of being the No. 1 pick in the 1994 Draft through sweat and determination, not just the ability with which he was born.

"People don't understand how hard that kid worked," Robinson's high school coach in Gary, Indiana, Ron Heflin, told *Sports Illustrated*. "He hasn't always been a polished player."

The improvement was noticeable when he made the varsity team by his sophomore year at Roosevelt High. From there, he led the team to a 73–7 record over the next three seasons, including an Indiana state championship in that basketball-crazy land. Robinson also won the state's top individual accolade: Mr. Basketball.

Just when you'd think he couldn't get any more popular in Indiana, Robinson decided to stay close to home to play at Purdue, located in West Lafayette. As in Gary, his career got off to a slow start when academic difficulties forced him to sit out his freshman season.

Robinson became depressed and almost quit school to return to Gary, where he had been born on January 10, 1973. He gained weight. Strangers approached him after class and kept asking how his grades were. It was a very tough time.

But the player who was nicknamed "Big Dog" by a custodian at Purdue stayed for two more seasons. That's all it took for him to become a star, and to be described by some as the most complete college star since another Indiana product, Larry Bird. He was named NCAA Player of the Year as a junior and, despite being a small forward, he became the first player to lead the Big Ten in rebounding and scoring in the same season since Minnesota's Mychal Thompson did it 16 years earlier.

When the Bucks won the NBA lottery, everyone figured Robinson was their man, not only a talented player but also a perfect fit with another top young Milwaukee prospect at power forward, Vin Baker. When the selection became official in June of 1994, Robinson became only the seventh early-entry candidate to go No. 1.

Robinson, a member of the 1996 Olympic team, made the All-Rookie Team in 1994-95 and averaged 21.9 points a game for 10th place in the league. Nobody could say he was dogging it.

Year	Team	G	FG	FG Pct.	FT	FT Pct.	Reb.	Ast.	TP	Avg.
1994-95	Milwaukee	80	636	.451	397	.796	513	197	1755	21.9

CHRIS WEBBER
Bullet on the Rise

It all came so fast to Chris Webber. He could dunk the ball in the seventh grade. In high school, he was such a celebrity he was signing autographs. At 21, he was already in the upper echelon of NBA stars.

Now, even bigger and better things are expected of the Washington Bullets' 6'10", 250-pound man-child. "I truly believe that he can be the best power forward in the game," said his former Golden State coach Don Nelson, now with the Knicks. "And I think he can be the best power forward ever."

It's not hard to get smitten by Webber, who in only two years in the NBA has already shown he's a spectacular dunker, nimble ball-handler, and terrific passer.

As the No. 1 overall pick in the 1993 Draft, Webber became the first NBA rookie to total at least 1,000 points, 500 rebounds, 250 assists, 150 blocks, and 75 steals.

That huge rookie season with Golden State helped quell any doubts that Webber was still depressed over committing one of basketball's most infamous bloopers. During the final seconds of the 1993 NCAA championship game against North Carolina, Webber instinctively called a timeout for his Michigan team . . . only Michigan didn't have any timeouts left. The Wolverines were whistled for a technical foul and lost their chance to beat the Tar Heels.

It seems Webber has always attracted attention. Born March 1, 1973, in Detroit, Michigan, the oldest of five children, Webber was chosen 1990-91 National Player of the Year when he starred at Detroit Country Day School. He entered Michigan as part of the celebrated "Fab Five," an entire team of flashy high school stars who entered Michigan together. Webber's play sparked the Wolverines to back-to-back appearances in the NCAA Championship game. In June 1993, he became the first sophomore selected as the No. 1 pick in the NBA Draft since Magic Johnson in 1979. Orlando drafted him and then dealt him to Golden State for No. 3 pick Anfernee Hardaway and three future first-round picks.

Webber fulfilled the Warriors' fondest wishes, blossoming into an immediate impact player with multiple skills. However, a clash with coach Nelson the next season prompted a surprising November 1994 trade to the Washington Bullets for Tom Gugliotta and three future draft picks.

In Washington, Webber was reunited with former Michigan teammate Juwan Howard, and the "Fab Two" are already laying the foundation for a bright future for the Bullets.

Year	Team	G	FG	FG Pct.	FT	FT Pct.	Reb.	Ast.	TP	Avg.
1993-94	Golden State	76	572	.552	189	.532	694	272	1333	17.5
1994-95	Washington	54	464	.495	117	.502	518	256	1085	20.1
	Totals	130	1036	.525	306	.520	1212	528	2418	18.6
	Playoff Totals	3	22	.550	3	.300	26	27	47	15.7

SCOTTIE PIPPEN
Prize Bull

Basketball never came easily for Scottie Pippen. Born September 25, 1965, in the tiny town of Hamburg, Arkansas, the youngest of 12 children, Pippen was on the frail side and showed little aptitude for the game. Even in high school, he didn't make the starting five until his senior year. And when his high-school coach got him a grant to attend Central Arkansas, Pippen's original intent was to serve as the team's equipment manager.

But by the time Pippen was a college senior, he had blossomed so incredibly that NBA scouts were following his every game.

The lean and lanky 6'7" guard-forward became the fifth overall pick of the 1987 Draft by the Seattle Sonics. But the Sonics traded him immediately to the Chicago Bulls for Olden Polynice and a No. 1 pick. And the late bloomer became a superstar.

The 210-pound Pippen swiftly established himself as a phenomenal defensive performer, his quickness enabling him to guard smaller players and his long arms permitting him to repulse bigger opponents. Though he has made the NBA's All-Defensive First

Team three times, he has become even better known as the perfect complement to Michael Jordan because of his amazing arsenal of offensive skills.

Pippen's supreme all-around game helped the Bulls win three NBA championships in a row—1991-92-93. And his versatility played a big role in the U.S. Dream Team's capture of a gold medal in the 1992 Olympics. Pippen is slated to be a member of the 1996 Olympic team, too.

A graceful, slashing player who runs the court as well as anybody in basketball, Pippen picked up the slack for the Bulls when Jordan left the game for $1\frac{1}{2}$ years. And in 1994-95, he did a pretty fair Air impression himself, leading Chicago in scoring, rebounding, assists, steals, and even blocked shots.

"This is a guy who has just moved up, up, up the ladder in our league," marveled former NBA coach Chuck Daly. "He truly has surfaced as one of the great players in the game."

Year	Team	G	FG	FG Pct.	FT	FT Pct.	Reb.	Ast.	TP	Avg.
1987-88	Chicago	79	261	.463	99	.576	298	169	625	7.9
1988-89	Chicago	73	413	.476	201	.668	445	256	1048	14.4
1989-90	Chicago	82	562	.489	199	.675	547	444	1351	16.5
1990-91	Chicago	82	600	.520	240	.706	595	511	1461	17.8
1991-92	Chicago	82	687	.506	330	.760	630	572	1720	21.0
1992-93	Chicago	81	628	.473	232	.663	621	507	1510	18.6
1993-94	Chicago	72	627	.491	270	.660	629	403	1587	22.0
1994-95	Chicago	79	634	.480	315	.716	639	409	1692	21.4
Totals		630	4412	.489	1886	.688	4404	3271	10994	17.5
Playoff Totals		120	823	.470	474	.727	934	631	2194	18.3

ALONZO MOURNING
"Zo" Good

Angry. Scowling. Raging. Why does Alonzo Mourning always give the impression he's about to explode?

"It's my intensity level on the floor," explained the 6'10", 240-pound center. "I want people to take me seriously. I'm trying as hard as I can for my team. The media think I'm an angry person, an out-of-control player. But I think my game thrives off intensity. That's all."

There's no question that Mourning plays basketball with a fierce determination. Just as there's no question he's one of the NBA's premier centers after three years with the Charlotte Hornets, and now with the Miami Heat. (Mourning was traded to the Heat for Glen Rice, Matt Geiger, Khalid Reeves, and a first-round 1996 draft pick just before the 1995–96 season began.)

A ferocious inside player with an increasingly effective perimeter shot, Mourning's game is frightening to opponents. But "Zo," as he's known, is downright scary defensively.

In his first season, Mourning was runner-up for Rookie of the Year to Orlando's Shaquille O'Neal. He was such an immediate force, he became the Hornets' all-time shot-blocker in only his 49th game! He finished the season with 271 blocks and has become the driving force behind Charlotte's fastbreaks.

"The thing about Zo is that he not only blocks shots, but he keeps them in play so we can have a chance to pick them up," said his teammate Larry Johnson. "We can't run if we don't stop somebody. But if we get the running going, it all breaks loose."

Born February 8, 1970, in Chesapeake, Virginia, Mourning was one of 49 foster children raised by an elderly woman named Fanny Threet. Other kids used to mock Mourning about being awkward and gangly and about his foster-care home, but he focused on school and developing his talent.

That talent blossomed at Georgetown, where he set an NCAA record for most career blocked shots (453) and became only the second player in Hoya history to score more than 2,000 points and grab 1,000 rebounds. The other player? Patrick Ewing.

The Hornets drafted him second overall in 1992. The first player? Shaquille O'Neal.

Mourning has never forgotten his tough childhood beginnings. He's active with youngsters in depressed Charlotte neighborhoods, and he serves as spokesman for a home for battered children. In these roles he's a far cry from the tough, explosive performer who put the buzz in the Hornets and now does it for Miami Heat.

Year	Team	G	FG	FG Pct.	FT	FT Pct.	Reb.	Ast.	TP	Avg.
1992-93	Charlotte..............	78	572	.511	495	.781	805	76	1639	21.0
1993-94	Charlotte..............	60	427	.505	433	.762	610	86	1287	21.5
1994-95	Charlotte..............	77	571	.519	490	.761	761	111	1643	21.3
	Totals	215	1570	.512	1418	.768	2176	273	4569	21.3
	Playoff Totals........................	13	95	.463	108	.794	142	24	302	23.2

BRAD DAUGHERTY
Riding High as a Cavalier

Brad Daugherty is not your average NBA center. Quick, name another big man who loves to go rattlesnake hunting and whose grandfather was a full-blooded Cherokee Indian.

Or one who grew seven inches in one year.

Born October 13, 1965, in Black Mountain, North Carolina, Daugherty's amazing growth spurt transformed him from 6'3" to 6'10" at age 12. He stopped growing thereafter, but was sufficiently skilled to play for the University of North Carolina as a 16-year-old freshman.

And he emerged as one of the best big men in Tar Heels history, his career 61.9 percent field-goal shooting breaking the school mark set by Bobby Jones.

Daugherty was so fundamentally sound—NBA scouts drooled over his smooth passing and pure shooting skills—the Cleveland Cavaliers made a deal to get him as the No. 1 player in the 1986 Draft.

In his first season, Daugherty was named to the All-Rookie team and quickly moved into the upper echelon of NBA centers. Unselfish, sometimes to a fault— "I'd rather pass than shoot the ball, to tell you the truth," Daugherty says—he has become the league's best passing big man. He led NBA centers in assists six times. And he's no slouch as a scorer, either, hitting an astounding 57 percent of his shots in 1991-92 and 1992-93. Only injuries have prevented him from reaching higher goals. A back ailment sidelined Daugherty at the beginning of the 1995-96 campaign and the Cavaliers weren't expecting him back on the court until at least halfway through the season.

Still, Daugherty is all-everything to the Cavaliers as their all-time leading scorer and all-time leading rebounder.

Year	Team	G	FG	FG Pct.	FT	FT Pct.	Reb.	Ast.	TP	Avg.
1986-87	Cleveland..............	80	487	.538	279	.696	647	304	1253	15.7
1987-88	Cleveland..............	79	551	.510	378	.716	665	333	1480	18.7
1988-89	Cleveland..............	78	544	.538	386	.737	718	285	1475	18.9
1989-90	Cleveland..............	41	244	.479	202	.704	373	130	690	16.8
1990-91	Cleveland..............	76	605	.524	435	.751	830	253	1645	21.6
1991-92	Cleveland..............	73	576	.570	414	.777	760	262	1566	21.5
1992-93	Cleveland..............	71	520	.571	391	.795	726	312	1432	20.2
1993-94	Cleveland..............	50	296	.488	256	.785	508	149	848	17.0
1994-95	Cleveland..............				Injured					
	Totals	548	3823	.532	2741	.747	5227	2028	10389	19.0
	Playoff Totals........................	41	275	.519	232	.756	419	137	782	19.1

KEVIN JOHNSON
A Gift for Giving

At 6'1", 190 pounds, he's the Phoenix Suns' little big man. He can shoot from the outside, penetrate almost at will, and dish to his teammates.

But for all the assists he gives to guys like Charles Barkley and Dan Majerle, perhaps Kevin Johnson's greatest gift is the one he gives to his old neighborhood in Sacramento, California.

"KJ," as he's known, created an after-school support program called St. Hope Academy for disadvantaged inner-city kids. The kids at St. Hope, according to administrator Pat Burks, "look up to Kevin as a big brother or father figure, not because he's a basketball player, but because of all the time he spends with them in the summer. They know he really cares."

Everyone knows KJ can really play basketball, too. "In terms of breaking down the defense and getting to the basket, he's one of the best," said Utah coach Jerry Sloan.

As the Suns' all-time assist leader (No. 14 on the all-time NBA list), Johnson is the fuel for Phoenix's high-powered engine. Four times he's made the All-NBA Second Team, and he's also one of the best playoff players in the league. In fact, KJ holds the NBA Finals single-game record for most minutes played—62, during a 1993 triple-overtime marathon against Chicago.

Born March 4, 1966, in Sacramento, Johnson was so fast as a youngster he was compared to a greyhound. He was also so good as a high-school shortstop, the Oakland A's selected him in the 1986 baseball draft. He even played a couple of minor-league games in the Oakland system.

But Johnson's future was in basketball. After starring at the University of California, he was selected by the Cleveland Cavaliers with the seventh pick in the 1987 Draft. In his rookie season, the Cavs traded him to Phoenix with Mark West and Tyrone Corbin for Larry Nance and Mike Sanders.

And the Suns have been shining brightly ever since.

Year	Team	G	FG	FG Pct.	FT	FT Pct.	Reb.	Ast.	TP	Avg.
1987-88	Clev.-Phoe	80	275	.461	177	.839	191	437	732	9.2
1988-89	Phoenix	81	570	.505	508	.882	340	991	1650	20.4
1989-90	Phoenix	74	578	.499	501	.838	270	846	1665	22.5
1990-91	Phoenix	77	591	.516	519	.843	271	781	1710	22.2
1991-92	Phoenix	78	539	.479	448	.807	292	836	1536	19.7
1992-93	Phoenix	49	282	.499	226	.819	104	384	791	16.1
1993-94	Phoenix	67	477	.487	380	.819	167	637	1340	20.0
1994-95	Phoenix	47	246	.470	234	.810	115	360	730	15.5
Totals		553	3558	.493	2993	.835	1750	5272	10154	18.4
Playoff Totals		83	617	.482	538	.834	288	820	1789	21.6

TIM HARDAWAY
The Bug Is Back

"Timmy just makes the game easy for everybody. He penetrates, gets guys shots, gets his own shots, plays defense, rebounds. He just does everything for us. And when the game is on the line, you have to wrestle him to get the ball." So says Golden State's Chris Mullin of teammate Tim Hardaway.

No one can refute Mullin's description. Especially after a 1994-95 season in which the 6-foot, 195-pound guard set a team record with 168 3-pointers and finished the season averaging 20.1 points and 9.3 assists, despite missing the final 20 games due to a wrist injury.

"Tim Bug," as he is known to his teammates, had reestablished himself as one of the league's toughest guards after being out for the entire 1993-94 season with a torn ligament in his left knee.

"When I'm on my game, I don't think anyone can defend me," says Hardaway. "Sometimes I feel like I'm the only one out there. Just by myself, like no one can stop me."

Hardaway was born September 1, 1966, in Chicago, where his father, Donald, was a playground legend and inspired him to pursue a life in basketball. Tim went on to become the all-time leading scorer at the University of Texas-El Paso and won the Naismith Basketball Hall of Fame Award as the nation's best collegian under 6 feet (he was 5'11" at the time).

Hardaway was taken by Golden State with the 14th pick in the 1989 NBA Draft and was an immediate success, making the All-NBA Rookie Team. His best season was 1991-92, when he averaged 23.4 points and 10.0 assists and was named to the All-NBA Third Team.

What makes Hardaway so tough? It's his cat-quick first step and a crossover dribble that ranks among the league's best. "As long as Tim has that crossover, he's the king because it can't be stopped," said former Los Angeles Lakers great Magic Johnson.

Now, Hardaway and the Warriors can only hope the injuries are a thing of the past.

Year	Team	G	FG	FG Pct.	FT	FT Pct.	Reb.	Ast.	TP	Avg.
1989-90	Golden State	79	464	.471	211	.764	310	689	1162	14.7
1990-91	Golden State	82	739	.476	306	.803	332	793	1881	22.9
1991-92	Golden State	81	734	.461	298	.766	310	807	1893	23.4
1992-93	Golden State	66	522	.447	273	.744	263	699	1419	21.5
1993-94	Golden State			Injured						
1994-95	Golden State	62	430	.427	219	.760	190	578	1247	20.1
	Totals	370	2889	.458	1307	.768	1405	3566	7602	20.5
	Playoff Totals	13	122	.460	54	.720	48	130	325	25.0

MAHMOUD ABDUL-RAUF
Pursuit of Perfection

Nobody is harder on Mahmoud Abdul-Rauf than . . . Mahmoud Abdul-Rauf. At the end of every practice session, he tells himself he must make 10 consecutive shots. For every one he misses, he must make two more before he leaves.

Sometimes when he makes a minor mistake during a game, Abdul-Rauf receives a real tongue-lashing . . . from Abdul-Rauf.

The Denver Nuggets' 6'1", 150-pound guard's drive for perfection—and his intolerance of imperfection—

stems from Tourette's syndrome, a neurological disorder that results in uncontrolled tics and vocal utterances.

It's a disorder that is painfully difficult to control, but Abdul-Rauf has certainly made the best of it. "I think Tourette's syndrome is a blessing because it enabled me to be a perfectionist," he said. "I didn't always think it was a blessing. When I was younger, I used to wonder what was wrong. It got so bad I just couldn't stop it, no matter how hard I tried. I'd finally just lie in bed and cry."

Born March 9, 1969, in Gulfport, Mississippi, Abdul-Rauf came into the world as Chris Jackson. But after converting to the Islam religion, he changed his name to Mahmoud Abdul-Rauf before the 1993-94 season.

At Louisiana State, Abdul-Rauf (then Jackson) made an instant name for himself when he scored 48 points in only his third college game, then topped that with a 53-point effort two games later. He led the tough Southeastern Conference in scoring in each of his two seasons, then turned pro after his sophomore year when he was selected third overall by the Nuggets in the 1990 NBA Draft.

His first two pro seasons were disappointments, but his iron will to succeed helped propel his ascent to stardom. In 1992-93, he improved his scoring from 10.3 to 19.2 points per game and was voted the league's Most Improved Player. In 1993-94, he made a stunning 95.6 percent of his foul shots—the second-highest percentage in NBA history, behind Calvin Murphy's 95.8—as he led the Nuggets in scoring for the second consecutive year.

One of the league's top sixth men in 1994-95, Abdul-Rauf's struggles with Tourette's syndrome and an endless pursuit of perfection nonetheless remain.

Year	Team	G	FG	FG Pct.	FT	FT Pct.	Reb.	Ast.	TP	Avg.
1990-91	Denver	67	417	.413	84	.857	121	206	942	14.1
1991-92	Denver	81	356	.421	94	.870	114	192	837	10.3
1992-93	Denver	81	633	.450	217	.935	225	344	1553	19.2
1993-94	Denver	80	588	.460	219	.956	168	362	1437	18.0
1994-95	Denver	73	472	.470	138	.885	137	263	1165	16.0
	Totals	382	2466	.445	752	.914	765	1367	5934	15.5
	Playoff. Totals	15	69	.369	43	.956	23	35	195	13.0

OTIS THORPE
The Percentage Shooter

It's not how many shots you take. It's how many baskets you make. And few players in the NBA can match Detroit's Otis Thorpe in this department.

He lost a second chance at a gold ring in 1994-95 when the Houston Rockets traded him on Valentine's Day to the Trail Blazers for Clyde Drexler and Tracy Murray. But this didn't deter him from finishing fourth in the league in field-goal percentage. No surprise here. Thorpe was third in 1993-94, the Rockets' first championship season, and fifth in 1992-93.

The 6'10", 246-pound power forward, respected for his rebounding skills as well as his shooting, was still going strong as he entered his 12th season in the NBA. Thorpe was traded to Detroit in September 1995.

The third youngest of 11 children, he was born August 5, 1962, in Boynton Beach, Florida. He was a late starter in high school, where he played only a year-and-a-half before enrolling at Providence College. There he finished as the Big East's career leader in rebounds and was second in scoring to Chris Mullin of St. John's.

"At first I hadn't really thought about playing pro ball," he said. "I was concentrating on graduating and getting into some kind of work. Then in my junior year I felt I could probably play in the NBA."

Thorpe was the ninth overall pick by the Kansas City (now Sacramento) Kings in 1984, and he soon became known as one of basketball's iron men. In his eleven seasons in the NBA, Thorpe has played in all but 29 games.

The Rockets made a winning deal when they got him in a trade for Rodney McCray and Jim Petersen in 1988. His career highlight came in the 1994 Finals against New York when he shot 27-for-53 for a .509 percentage as Houston won the title.

Thorpe doesn't get as many headlines as other superstars, but as his former Rocket teammate Kenny Smith says, "When you get the ball to Otis, he's either going to score or make the pass that will get you a basket."

Year	Team	G	FG	FG Pct.	FT	FT Pct.	Reb.	Ast.	TP	Avg.
1984-85	Kansas City	82	411	.600	230	.620	556	111	1052	12.8
1985-86	Sacramento	75	289	.587	164	.661	420	84	742	9.9
1986-87	Sacramento	82	567	.540	413	.761	819	201	1547	18.9
1987-88	Sacramento	82	622	.507	460	.755	837	266	1704	20.8
1988-89	Houston	82	521	.542	328	.729	787	202	1370	16.7
1989-90	Houston	82	547	.548	307	.688	734	261	1401	17.1
1990-91	Houston	82	549	.556	334	.696	846	197	1435	17.5
1991-92	Houston	82	558	.592	304	.657	862	250	1420	17.3
1992-93	Houston	72	385	.558	153	.598	589	181	923	12.8
1993-94	Houston	82	449	.561	251	.657	870	189	1149	14.0
1994-95	Hou.-Port.	70	385	.565	167	.594	558	112	937	13.4
Totals		873	5283	.555	3111	.687	7878	2054	13680	15.7
Playoff Totals		52	272	.587	124	.626	434	114	669	12.9

MITCH RICHMOND
Power to the King

Throughout his life, Mitch Richmond was very close to his grandmother, a loving woman who was like a second mother to him. So when Emma Thomas died at age 69, a few months before the 1995 NBA All-Star Game, Richmond dedicated the game to her memory.

That memory stirred the Sacramento Kings' guard to one of the most sensational performances in All-Star Game history. Richmond scored 23 points in 22 minutes, becoming the first reserve to win Most Valuable Player honors since Tiny Archibald in 1981.

Born June 30, 1965, in Fort Lauderdale, Florida, Richmond developed into a powerful athlete, starring in football as well as basketball at Boyd Anderson High. One of his football teammates was Michael Irvin, now a star receiver for the Dallas Cowboys. While Irvin was setting pass-catching records, Richmond turned into a tenacious defensive back. But basketball was his true love.

He played two years at Mobley (Kansas) Junior College before starring at Kansas State, where he became a second-team All-American averaging 20.7 points a game. He also won a bronze medal as a member of the U.S. basketball team at the 1988 Olympics in Seoul, Korea.

After the Golden State Warriors made the 6'5", 215-pounder the fifth pick in the 1988 Draft, Richmond exceeded many expectations. Besides showing a deft shooting touch, he also overpowered veteran NBA guards with his remarkable strength and was named Rookie of the Year. Richmond's bruising, tough style of play inspired teammates to call him "Rock" and "Hammer." He had three productive years with Golden State before being dealt to Sacramento in 1991 for the rights to Billy Owens, the Kings' top draftee.

"One of the best shooters around," Seattle Sonics coach George Karl said of Richmond. "And he's got all that strength to get inside and score."

Year	Team	G	FG	FG Pct.	FT	FT Pct.	Reb.	Ast.	TP	Avg.
1988-89	Golden State	79	649	.468	410	.810	468	334	1741	22.0
1989-90	Golden State	78	640	.497	406	.866	360	223	1720	22.1
1990-91	Golden State	77	703	.494	394	.847	452	238	1840	23.9
1991-92	Sacramento	80	685	.468	330	.813	319	411	1803	22.5
1992-93	Sacramento	45	371	.474	197	.845	154	221	987	21.9
1993-94	Sacramento	78	635	.445	426	.834	286	313	1823	23.4
1994-95	Sacramento	82	668	.446	375	.843	357	311	1867	22.8
Totals		519	4351	.469	2538	.836	2396	2051	11781	22.7
Playoff Totals		17	147	.484	57	.919	105	57	362	21.3

LARRY JOHNSON
Sting of a Hornet

Watching a 6'7", 250-pound hulking forward station himself a long way from the basket is not a common sight. But then Larry Johnson is not a common basketball player. "Larry Johnson's 3-point shooting is something to behold," marveled Charlotte Hornets assistant coach John Bach. "It's like there's a linebacker from 35 feet out, pumping away. And at times, it's a nail in someone's coffin."

Indeed, Johnson, the Hornets' bruising power forward with an already explosive game, is finding new ways to bury opponents. In 1994-95, he connected on almost three times as many 3-pointers (81) as in his previous three seasons combined (28).

Long before Johnson showed his new offensive punch, though, he was delivering punches. From the time he was 9 until he was 13, Johnson loved to box in the Police Athletic League in Dallas, where he grew up. But he discovered basketball and quickly became a playground legend.

Born March 14, 1969, in Tyler, Texas, Johnson starred at Skyline High School in Dallas and, as a senior, was voted "most likely to succeed" by his classmates.

Succeed he did—first at Nevada-Las Vegas, where he led the Runnin' Rebels to the NCAA championship in 1990 and was named College Player of the Year in 1991.

Then, when the Hornets made him the No. 1 overall pick in the 1991 Draft, he roared into the NBA and won Rookie of the Year honors. The next year, he led Charlotte in scoring and rebounding, and became a starter in the All-Star Game, the first Hornet ever to make the team. Johnson also became renowned for his humorous portrayal as "Grandmama" in a sneaker commercial.

Brash and confident, Johnson is all business on the court. He doesn't care about the size of the man between him and the basket. If he can't go over him, he'll go through him. Or just step behind the 3-point line and burn him.

Year	Team	G	FG	FG Pct.	FT	FT Pct.	Reb.	Ast.	TP	Avg.
1991-92	Charlotte..............	82	616	.490	339	.829	899	292	1576	19.2
1992-93	Charlotte..............	82	728	.526	336	.767	864	353	1810	22.1
1993-94	Charlotte..............	51	346	.515	137	.695	448	184	834	16.4
1994-95	Charlotte..............	81	585	.480	274	.774	585	369	1525	18.8
	Totals	296	2275	.502	1086	.777	2796	1198	5745	19.4
	Playoff Totals.......................	13	99	.529	61	.701	85	41	261	20.1

KENNY ANDERSON
Dynamo at the Point

When watching Kenny Anderson, many NBA people see similarities to another New York City schoolboy legend.

"He reminds me of Tiny Archibald," said veteran forward Rick Mahorn, referring to the Hall of Fame point guard. "Left-handed, using people on the pick-and-rolls, he's like another coming of Tiny."

A slender 6'1", 170-pounder, Anderson has become one of the NBA's most exciting and flashiest young players. Born October 9, 1970, in Queens, New York, he grew up in a housing project and developed his game on the most challenging playgrounds on the planet. It's also where he developed a special toughness.

That grit has served him well in the pros, where he broke his left wrist after a collision with the Knicks' John Starks in 1993. Despite another painful break in the wrist the following season, Anderson still managed to play in 72 games.

Anderson's court vision is expansive. Few point guards can score and distribute the ball so effortlessly.

In fact, he led all NBA point guards in 1993-94 in scoring (18.8 points per game), while his 9.6 assists were the league's fourth-best overall.

Great things were always expected of Anderson, who's still known as "The Kid," just as he was when he drew national attention playing for Archbishop Molloy High School. He starred at Georgia Tech for two years, averaging 25.9 points per game as a sophomore, before deciding to turn pro. Though the Nets selected him second overall in the 1991 Draft, Anderson didn't see eye-to-eye with then-coach Bill Fitch. So Anderson gathered a lot of splinters on the bench.

But it all turned around in 1992-93 when Chuck Daly became the coach and turned Anderson loose. And the dynamic point guard has been on the ascent ever since.

Year	Team	G	FG	FG Pct.	FT	FT Pct.	Reb.	Ast.	TP	Avg.
1991-92	New Jersey	64	187	.390	73	.745	127	203	450	7.0
1992-93	New Jersey	55	370	.435	180	.776	226	449	927	16.9
1993-94	New Jersey	82	576	.417	346	.818	322	784	1538	18.8
1994-95	New Jersey	72	411	.399	348	.841	250	680	1267	17.6
Totals		273	1544	.413	947	.811	925	2116	4182	15.3
Playoff Totals		7	22	.349	24	.686	15	30	71	10.1

MARK PRICE
Always on the Mark

Not all the gushing in the oil country of Enid, Oklahoma, came from the town's many oil rigs. A skinny high-school sophomore guard named Mark Price caused plenty of gushing himself.

Perfecting his ball-handling skills and eagle-eye shooting during intense pickup games with his younger brothers, Price elevated his high-school team to new heights. He led an undersized Enid squad to the 1982 Oklahoma state finals and became such a heroic figure that the town eventually renamed its gym "Mark Price Arena."

Born February 15, 1964, in Bartlesville, Oklahoma, Price attended Georgia Tech, where he became the school's No. 2 all-time scorer. However, doubts followed him. With his choirboy looks and small size (6 feet, 178 pounds), many pro scouts felt he wasn't NBA material. The Dallas Mavericks selected him in the second round (25th overall) of the 1986 Draft, but had no intention of keeping him. They traded him to Cleveland for a future pick and cash, but Price quickly made the Mavs regret it.

Not only did he become the heart and soul of the Cavaliers, he became one of the best players in team history.

As Cleveland's floor general, Price was impeccable at penetrating, finding the open man, and finding his own spots to unleash long-range missiles. He made the All-NBA First Team in 1992-93 and played for the USA Dream Team in the 1994 World Championship in Toronto. A deadly sharpshooter, he holds the NBA record for free-throw percentage (.906). The Washington Bullets were looking for more of the same when they acquired him in a trade prior to the 1995-96 season.

"The thing that makes Mark so tough is that he's got one of the fastest releases in the game," said Phil Jackson, the Chicago Bulls' coach. "He's lightning quick."

Year	Team	G	FG	FG Pct.	FT	FT Pct.	Reb.	Ast.	TP	Avg.
1986-87	Cleveland	67	173	.408	95	.833	117	202	464	6.9
1987-88	Cleveland	80	493	.506	221	.877	180	480	1279	16.0
1988-89	Cleveland	75	529	.526	263	.901	226	631	1414	18.9
1989-90	Cleveland	73	489	.459	300	.888	251	666	1430	19.6
1990-91	Cleveland	16	97	.497	59	.952	45	166	271	16.9
1991-92	Cleveland	72	438	.488	270	.947	173	535	1247	17.3
1992-93	Cleveland	75	477	.484	289	.948	201	602	1365	18.2
1993-94	Cleveland	76	480	.478	238	.888	228	589	1316	17.3
1994-95	Cleveland	48	253	.413	148	.914	112	335	757	15.8
Totals		582	3429	.479	1883	.906	1533	4206	9543	16.4
Playoff Totals		47	280	.464	202	.944	124	327	818	17.4

GARY PAYTON
Spirit of Seattle

He's lightning-quick, a dazzling passer and penetrator, and a supreme scorer. However, Gary Payton's main objective is no longer offensive. "One of my ultimate goals is to be the Defensive Player of the Year," says the Seattle Sonics' tenacious 6'4", 190-pound guard. "It's the only goal I really care about other than winning the championship."

If not the best point guard in the NBA, Payton is the best on-the-ball defender. His long arms and quickness make life miserable for opposing guards. "Payton's defense is awesome," said former Boston Celtics great K.C. Jones, a defensive stalwart himself. Indeed, in 1993-94, only his fourth season as a pro, Payton was voted onto the NBA's All-Defensive First Team. And he made it again in 1994-95.

Born July 23, 1968, in Oakland, California, Payton grew up rooting for the Oakland A's and was a star shortstop on the Skyline High School team, as well as a standout in basketball. He attended Oregon State, where his brilliant basketball wizardry enabled him to become the school's all-time leading scorer and rank second on the all-time NCAA lists in steals and assists. As a senior in 1990, *Sports Illustrated* named him College Player of the Year, and the Sonics made him the second pick overall of the 1990 Draft.

Known for his brash, nonstop talking on court— "Get somebody out here who can guard me!" Payton used to yell at opposing benches in college—he has recently toned down his act. He has emerged as a respected team leader on the Sonics and has only missed one game in his five NBA seasons.

But despite cutting down the trash-talking, Payton hasn't let up on harassing opponents as basketball's most relentless on-the-ball defender.

Year	Team	G	FG	FG Pct.	FT	FT Pct.	Reb.	Ast.	TP	Avg.
1990-91	Seattle	82	259	.450	69	.711	243	528	588	7.2
1991-92	Seattle	81	331	.451	99	.669	295	506	764	9.4
1992-93	Seattle	82	476	.494	151	.770	281	399	1110	13.5
1993-94	Seattle	82	584	.504	166	.595	269	494	1349	16.5
1994-95	Seattle	82	685	.509	249	.716	281	583	1689	20.6
	Totals	409	2335	.489	734	.687	1369	2510	5500	13.4
	Playoff Totals	41	208	.456	47	.573	124	189	469	11.4

SHAWN BRADLEY
Standing Tall

Shawn Bradley stands 7'6" and weighs 248 pounds, so he looks like an exclamation point. This is fitting, though, because his basketball career has been full of excitement.

He was 7'5" while starring in high school in Castle Dale, Utah, but certainly not a gangly geek. It took only a brief look to tell that Bradley was coordinated beyond his years, seemingly more able to work within his unusual body than an NBA player like, say, 7'7" Manute Bol. He was not just some big guy.

Bradley could have gone to college anywhere, but picked Brigham Young in nearby Provo because of his Mormon faith. Once there, the only question was how long he would stay.

Bradley, already very mature for his age, led the NCAA in shot-blocking as a 19-year-old freshman and tied the record for the most swats in a game when he got an astounding 14 against Eastern Kentucky. He also averaged 14.8 points, a nice contribution on its own. Then he left for two years—to do Mormon missionary work in Australia.

The big decision came next. Bradley had a total of 34 games worth of experience in college, but that did not deter him from announcing he would turn pro.

The Orlando Magic had the first pick in the 1993 Draft and took Chris Webber. Philadelphia went next. The 76ers needed a center, but there was some debate whether Bradley was too weak or too unpolished to ever develop into a star. Point guard Anfernee Hardaway would have been a much safer choice.

Undaunted, the 76ers took Bradley and then made an even bigger commitment: a $44-million contract. He missed about half the 1993-94 season due to injury, but made the All-Rookie Second Team. The consensus was still split. Some believed he showed enough flashes of greatness to justify the selection, while others figured he would be a bust.

"I've said from Day 1 that I lack experience," Bradley said. "But I've also said that as I gain experience, I'll become a better player."

He is the tallest American ever to play in the NBA, and also one of the most scrutinized. The 76ers got him a couple of special tutors—Kareem Abdul-Jabbar to improve his basketball skills and former Mr. Olympia Lee Haney to improve his strength. Bradley responded in his second season, 1994-95, with the same roller-coaster ride of greatness and mediocrity. But he made maximum use of his height to rank third in blocked-shot average in the league, behind Denver's Dikembe Mutombo and Houston's Hakeem Olajuwon.

Will he make it? It won't be hard to find out. He is, after all, impossible to miss.

Year	Team	G	FG	FG Pct.	FT	FT Pct.	Reb.	Ast.	TP	Avg.
1993-94	Philadelphia	49	201	.409	102	.607	306	98	504	10.3
1994-95	Philadelphia	82	315	.455	148	.638	659	53	778	9.5
	Totals	131	516	.436	250	.625	965	151	1282	9.8

JIM JACKSON
Mavs' Secret Weapon

Jim Jackson doesn't get a lot of publicity. In his first full season, 1992-93, the Dallas Mavericks' guard averaged 19.2 points but was overshadowed on his own team by rookie Jamal Mashburn. Then in 1994-95, his 25.7 scoring average was the highest in the league by any guard, and still people talked more about the impressive play of his rookie teammate Jason Kidd.

But although Jackson may be the league's best-kept secret, the coaches around the league have noticed him. "What is there not to like about him?" Hawks coach Lenny Wilkens said. "He can go outside or inside, he pushes the ball, he can defend."

At 6'6", 220 pounds, Jackson is big enough to overpower most guards, so some teams try to defend with a small forward. But Jackson's quickness and ball-handling ability make that a very tough assignment, even for the NBA's fastest forwards.

Born October 14, 1970, in Toledo, Ohio, Jackson starred in both basketball and football as a youth. He twice took Macomber High School to the state championship and was selected as Ohio's "Mr. Basketball."

Jackson concentrated solely on basketball once he got to Ohio State, and the move paid off. He led the Buckeyes to three straight NCAA tournament appearances and back-to-back Big Ten titles, and was named an All-American after averaging 22.4 points his junior season.

He left school at the end of that semester and was taken by the Mavericks with the fourth pick in the 1992 Draft. After a lengthy holdout due to a contract dispute, Jackson joined the Mavericks March 5, 1993, and played the final 28 games of the regular season. He averaged 16.3 points and showed signs of brilliance down the stretch, scoring 20 or more points in each of the Mavs' last seven games.

He increased his scoring by nearly three points per game in 1993-94 and was up to 25.7 before a badly sprained ankle forced him out of the final 31 games of 1994-95.

Year	Team	G	FG	FG Pct.	FT	FT Pct.	Reb.	Ast.	TP	Avg.
1992-93	Dallas	28	184	.395	68	.739	122	131	457	16.3
1993-94	Dallas	82	637	.445	285	.821	388	374	1576	19.2
1994-95	Dallas	51	484	.472	306	.805	260	191	1309	25.7
	Totals	161	1305	.446	659	.805	770	696	3342	20.8

VLADE DIVAC
The Proud Laker

It wasn't too long ago that when people talked about imports coming to the United States from Europe, they meant cars or musicians. Then came the late 1980s and the NBA started to reach across the Atlantic Ocean.

The Los Angeles Lakers' haul was a 7'1", 250-pound center named Vlade Divac, who would quickly prove very likeable as a person, but very frustrating as a player because he was often inconsistent. Teammates like Magic Johnson and James Worthy questioned his mental approach, and on a club where anything less than the championship was considered failure, that didn't sit well.

Now, that all seems so long ago. Not only has Divac emerged as one of the leaders of the new Lakers, but as one of the better centers in the league. He's gone from being a Yugoslavian with a lot to prove to an NBA standout with a lot to be proud of.

"I'm a Yugoslavian who loves America—my kids are Americans, you know," he says proudly. "They're always going to be half-and-half because they were born here and, I hope, live here, but they will always have a background of Yugoslavian. I'm still a Serbian, but with an American lifestyle."

Divac was born February 3, 1968, in the town of Prijepolje and was good enough in basketball to get an offer to move to another city, Kraljevo, to play with more advanced players even though he was still quite young. He accepted. Soon, he developed friendships with Drazen Petrovic (who would play with the Trail Blazers and Nets), Toni Kukoc (Bulls), and Dino Radja (Celtics), and he became an important part of the Yugoslavian Olympic team that won a silver medal in 1988 in Seoul, Korea.

A year later, the Lakers drafted him 26th. He played against Petrovic and Lithuanian-born Sarunas Marciulionis (Sacramento) in the NBA. Kukoc and Radja weren't far behind. When civil war broke out in Yugoslavia, Divac was adamant about not getting caught in the political ramifications, so he held fund-raisers for kids of all backgrounds in his native country, not just Serbians like himself.

He has persevered through this difficult time to become someone the Lakers can count on, someone who is usually good for double-figure rebounds and points. Someone who the fans of Los Angeles are happy to call their own.

Year	Team	G	FG	FG Pct.	FT	FT Pct.	Reb.	Ast.	TP	Avg.
1989-90	L.A. Lakers	82	274	.499	153	.708	512	75	701	8.5
1990-91	L.A. Lakers	82	360	.565	196	.703	666	92	921	11.2
1991-92	L.A. Lakers	36	157	.495	86	.768	247	60	405	11.3
1992-93	L.A. Lakers	82	397	.485	235	.689	729	232	1050	12.8
1993-94	L.A. Lakers	79	453	.506	208	.686	851	307	1123	14.2
1994-95	L.A. Lakers	80	485	.507	297	.777	829	329	1277	16.0
	Totals	441	2126	.509	1175	.720	3834	1095	5477	12.4
	Playoff Totals	47	238	.523	135	.734	329	105	619	13.2

A BARREL OF HOOPS
Fantastic Finishes

━━ ━━ ━━

The clock is winding down to the final seconds in a close game. The spectators are on their feet. Who's going to win?

The 1995 NBA playoffs had a number of spectacular games that went down to the wire. Here's a recap of those breathtakers:

April 27—John Stockton scores on a layup with 2.4 seconds remaining to give Utah a 102-100 victory over Houston.

May 7—In the last 18.7 seconds, Indiana's Reggie Miller scores eight points, including two free throws with 7.5 seconds left, enabling the Pacers to edge the Knicks, 107-105.

May 16—With 0.5 seconds remaining in overtime, Nick Van Exel's 3-pointer is the difference as the Lakers beat San Antonio, 115-114.

May 17—There are only 1.8 seconds to go when the Knicks' Patrick Ewing drives the lane to stop Indiana, 96-95.

May 20—Mario Elie sinks a 3-pointer with 7.1 seconds

left to give Houston a 115-114 series-clinching victory over Phoenix.

May 22—The clock shows 6.4 seconds remaining when Robert Horry hits on a 17-footer, his only field goal of the game, as Houston nips San Antonio, 94-93.

May 29—No time left when Indiana's Rik Smits nets a 14-footer for a 94-93 win over Orlando. The game had four lead changes in the final 13.3 seconds.

June 7—It's overtime in Game 1 of the Finals. With three-tenths of a second to go, Houston's Hakeem Olajuwon tips one in for a 120-118 victory over Orlando.

June 11—With 14 seconds left in Game 3 of the Finals, Houston's Robert Horry nails a 3-pointer for a 104-100 lead. But Orlando's Nick Anderson counters with a 3-pointer to bring the Magic within range with just 2.7 seconds remaining. But the Rockets hold on for a 106-103 victory.

Cal Ripken's Passion for Basketball

Cal Ripken, the great Baltimore Oriole shortstop who broke Lou Gehrig's record for the most consecutive games in 1995, loves to play basketball.

He does it in the off-season at home in a dream gymnasium so big it has almost everything—a batting cage, weight-lifting equipment, an oscillating tennis-ball machine that feeds him grounders, a trampoline, and, of course, a basketball court.

A man with a huge competitive drive, Ripken brings in an assortment of players—active collegians, former college and pro players, and Oriole teammates. They have fun, but these are serious games and more often than not, Ripken is on the winning team. He actually keeps scouting reports on all the players who perform in his gym.

According to *Sports Illustrated,* he uses official Spalding NBA *game balls*—balls that have been sent to him by NBA teams.

Growing up in Aberdeen, Maryland, Ripken played baseball and soccer. Basketball? Well, he's proving it's never too late to take up another sport, especially on your home court.

Jogging with the President

What does it take to get an invitation from the President of the United States?

Well, you could try basketball. That's how Rebecca Lobo did it. Rebecca happens to have been a 6'4" forward on the University of Connecticut team that she led to a 35-0 record and the national championship in 1994-95.

Rebecca was a guest on "The Late Show with David Letterman" and had a shoot-around with Harry Smith on "CBS This Morning." And she soon had promotional contracts with Spalding and Reebok.

She missed graduation and her team's visit to the White House with President Clinton because she was busy earning a spot on the U.S. national team. But Rebecca got a second chance with the President. He invited her to go jogging. They did it for three miles near the Potomac River. She knew when to slow down.

"He was setting the pace," she said. "I wasn't about to run away from the President."

Close Call

It happened on a chartered flight the Minneapolis Lakers were taking from St. Louis to Minnesota on the night of January 17, 1960. They were aboard the DC-3 purchased by club owner Bob Short.

Shortly after takeoff, the electrical system failed. The pilot, flying without lights or a radio, was guided by a magnetic compass. But the plane drifted off course and the aircraft, low on fuel, had to find a place to land, guided only by the lights of a small town in western Iowa.

When news of the missing flight was reported on the radio back in Minneapolis, injured forward Steve Hamilton, who had stayed behind, feared he was the only surviving Laker.

After being in the air five hours, the occupants of the plane—including Elgin Baylor, Rudy LaRusso, and "Hot Rod" Hundley—all returned safely. The DC-3 had to land in a field, where the plane slid about 100 yards but suffered no major damage.

"I had not been scared in the least when we were in the air or when we were landing," recalled Lakers coach Jim Pollard, whose mode of transportation back to town turned out to be a hearse driven by a local mortician. "But when I saw that stretcher in the back of the hearse, I realized how close we had come. Then I got the shakes for a few minutes."

"Put the Ball in the Basket"

Players have to be careful about what they say to referees in the heat of battle. Or at any time. They can draw a technical foul, get thrown out of a game, or be fined.

A referee has to watch himself as well. Take the case of Charley Eckman, who refereed in the NBA in the early 1950s. He was one of the officials at a game in the 1953-54 season in which the Minneapolis Lakers beat the Fort Wayne Pistons. Later, in a restaurant, Eckman told Lakers star George Mikan, "If I were coaching the Pistons, I'd beat you."

Fred Zollner, the Pistons' owner, heard about the comment. When he needed a coach for the 1954-55 season, he gave the job to Eckman, who had never coached at any level of basketball.

Was it a disaster? Hardly. In his very first year, the Pistons won the Western Division title. They went on to reach the NBA Finals, only to lose by a point to the Syracuse Nationals in Game 7.

After coaching for three-plus seasons, Eckman became an announcer. He's the fellow who once said, "There are only two great plays—*South Pacific* and put the ball in the basket."

The Dream Team

It all began with the 1992 Olympic Games in Barcelona, Spain. For the first time, the U.S. team was represented by professionals—NBA players. And they were rightly called the "Dream Team."

What a lineup! Michael Jordan, Magic Johnson, Patrick Ewing, Larry Bird, Charles Barkley, Clyde Drexler, Karl Malone, Chris Mullin, Scottie Pippen, David Robinson, and John Stockton. Plus one collegian, Duke's Christian Laettner. The head coach was Chuck Daly, then coach of the Detroit Pistons.

How could they lose? They didn't. The U.S. breezed to the winners' circle, erasing memories of the 1988 Olympics in Seoul, Korea, in which they had to settle for a bronze medal as the third-place team behind the Soviet Union and Yugoslavia.

That was the year that the U.S. played with future NBA stars David Robinson, Mitch Richmond, Dan Majerle, Willie Anderson, and Danny Manning.

In all of Olympic basketball history, starting in 1936, the U.S. has compiled an unbelievable 90-2 record. Uncle Sam's only other setback came in 1972 at Munich, Germany, when the Soviets won after being given an extra three seconds in a controversial game.

Another Dream Team

Another powerful Dream Team surfaced in the 1994 World Championships at Toronto. As in the '92 Olympics, NBA players competed as members of the U.S. team. In the lineup were Majerle, Shaq O'Neal, Reggie Miller, Dominique Wilkins, Joe Dumars, Alonzo Mourning, Mark Price, Shawn Kemp, Derrick Coleman, Larry Johnson, Kevin Johnson, and Steve Smith.

It was a runaway. The U.S. captured the title with an 8-0 record, capped by the 137-91 triumph over Russia. O'Neal, Miller, and Kemp made the All-Tournament Team.

And now it's time for yet another Dream Team, which will play in the 1996 Olympic Games in Atlanta. Holdovers from the '92 team are Karl Malone, Scottie Pippen, John Stockton, and David Robinson. The others, making their Olympic debut, are O'Neal, Miller, Hakeem Olajuwon, Anfernee Hardaway, Grant Hill, and Glenn Robinson.

Nobody could be better suited to coach the team than Lenny Wilkens, coach of the host city Atlanta Hawks and holder of the NBA record as its winningest coach.

NBA Around the World

They speak NBA everywhere. The league's international appeal is such that the 1995 NBA Finals were viewed on television in 164 countries on 6 continents in 40 different languages.

Radio broadcasts in the United States also reflect the interest of our country's foreign-born fans. In Los Angeles, Clippers games are heard in Chinese and you can follow, in their respective cities, the games of Chicago, Golden State, Houston, Miami, Denver, Phoenix, and San Antonio in Spanish. And if you're a Navajo Indian, you can hear the play-by-play action in your language on a radio station in Phoenix.

French Canadians are, of course, likely to follow the newest teams in the NBA—the Toronto Raptors and Vancouver Grizzlies—in 1995-96.

The game translates into excitement in any language.

Hoop Dodger

Imagine Tommy Lasorda with a whistle in his mouth.

He needs no introduction to baseball fans or to the world of television viewers who are constantly exposed to his diet food commercials.

Few know, however, that there's a basketball in his background. Before the longtime Los Angeles Dodgers manager was chosen to lead the team in 1977, he was a referee in the Eastern Basketball League (now the Continental Basketball Association).

Following a mostly minor-league pitching career (he did appear in 29 games with the Dodgers in 1957), Lasorda worked as an EBL official in 1961, 1962, and part of 1963.

He went full-time with the Dodger organization after that, but remains a faithful follower of pro basketball.

Teddy Bear Trouble

The girls' basketball team at Burrton High School in Burrton, Kansas, was ruled ineligible for competition in 1991 because the players took gifts from supporters: teddy bears that were three inches high and worth $1.

The girls had been given the teddy bears at a dinner celebrating their fourth-place finish in a state tournament.

The Kansas State High School Athletic Association said the bears violated a rule prohibiting students from accepting cash or merchandise from the school or boosters. The association said there would be no more basketball for the girls unless they returned the bears.

"If we were trying to bribe the girls, we would bribe them with something more than a dollar bear," said Joyce Boyle, one of the dinner's organizers.

The girls reluctantly gave up the bears.

TESTING...1...2...3

▬ ▬ ▬

Here's something to do during a time-out—when you don't want to watch another commercial. And nobody's going to give you a bad mark if you don't know the answers.

Answers begin on page 269.

Who's Calling the Shots?

Match the NBA team with its 1995-96 head coach.

1. Boston Celtics
2. New York Knicks
3. Detroit Pistons
4. Toronto Raptors
5. Denver Nuggets
6. Vancouver Grizzlies
7. Golden State Warriors

a. Doug Collins
b. Brendan Malone
c. Rick Adelman
d. Don Nelson
e. Brian Winters
f. M.L. Carr
g. Bernie Bickerstaff

Who's Who in Scoring

Match the 1994-95 team scoring leader with his team.

1. Dominique Wilkins
2. Alonzo Mourning
3. Glenn Robinson
4. Cedric Ceballos
5. Chris Webber
6. Gary Payton
7. Mitch Richmond
8. Mookie Blaylock
9. Latrell Sprewell
10. Loy Vaught

a. Milwaukee Bucks
b. Washington Bullets
c. Boston Celtics
d. Los Angeles Clippers
e. Atlanta Hawks
f. Charlotte Hornets
g. Golden State Warriors
h. Sacramento Kings
i. Seattle Sonics
j. Los Angeles Lakers

The College Connection

Match the NBA superstar with his college.

1. David Robinson
2. Patrick Ewing
3. Glenn Robinson
4. Hakeem Olajuwon
5. Mitch Richmond
6. Shaquille O'Neal
7. Derrick Coleman
8. Grant Hill
9. Michael Jordan
10. John Stockton

a. University of Houston
b. Gonzaga
c. Kansas State
d. Duke
e. U.S. Naval Academy
f. Purdue
g. Syracuse
h. North Carolina
i. Georgetown
j. Louisiana State

Know Your Colors

Match each NBA team with its colors.

1. Dallas Mavericks
2. Denver Nuggets
3. Chicago Bulls
4. Houston Rockets
5. Los Angeles Lakers
6. Boston Celtics
7. Orlando Magic
8. Charlotte Hornets
9. Indiana Pacers
10. Vancouver Grizzlies

a. Red, white, and black
b. Turquoise, bronze, and red
c. Green and white
d. Teal, purple, and white
e. Gold, blue, and red
f. Blue, silver, and black
g. Blue and yellow
h. Red and gold
i. Blue and green
j. Royal purple and gold

There's No Place Like Home

Match the NBA team with its home arena.

1. Indiana
2. Minnesota
3. San Antonio
4. Denver
5. New York
6. Milwaukee
7. Chicago
8. Atlanta
9. Houston
10. Sacramento
11. Detroit
12. Dallas

a. The Palace of Auburn Hills
b. United Center
c. Reunion Arena
d. ARCO Arena
e. McNichols Sports Arena
f. Target Center
g. Bradley Center
h. The Summit
i. Market Square Arena
j. The Omni
k. Madison Square Garden
l. The Alamodome

Superstar Search

Find the NBA superstars in the maze. The stars' last names will read up, down, across, or diagonally. Check the names off on the list below as you find them.

```
F  R  E  Y  R  R  O  H  G  T  P  P  M
O  I  D  M  O  G  F  C  I  T  O  N  A
L  L  G  E  N  C  R  N  S  O  U  R  L
K  G  A  I  A  F  X  P  I  C  N  U  O
C  G  W  J  S  T  A  R  K  S  U  B  N
O  E  L  A  U  E  P  A  C  R  G  H  E
L  I  M  K  E  W  E  P  U  N  I  S  H
Y  N  Y  A  G  E  O  X  I  L  V  A  N
A  W  M  A  L  S  E  N  L  O  A  M  O
L  P  O  P  W  B  N  L  A  C  G  X  O
B  E  L  O  V  A  N  D  U  K  E  M  P
N  O  R  N  M  A  D  E  C  D  E  R  S
A  D  N  E  W  I  F  R  R  I  D  E  R
D  A  R  F  K  O  N  E  A  L  E  F  E
R  P  E  E  O  F  O  B  T  H  E  S  H
O  R  L  E  X  E  N  A  V  R  C  B  T
J  I  L  A  R  L  B  D  R  I  D  W  A
U  C  I  G  W  I  E  Y  I  N  W  X  E
P  E  M  Y  E  L  K  R  A  B  C  E  W
```

Barkley	Hill	O'Neal
Blaylock	Horry	Price
Drexler	Jordan	Rider
Ewing	Malone	Scott
Ferry	Manning	Starks
Kemp	Mashburn	Van Exel
Kidd	Miller	Weatherspoon
Hardaway	Olajuwon	

YESTERDAY'S HEROES

▬ ▬ ▬

Isiah Thomas is here. So are Larry Bird, Magic Johnson, and Kareem Abdul-Jabbar. It was only yesterday, or not much before, that they were making headlines. And now they're retired. But there is no forgetting these legendary players and their amazing achievements.

KAREEM ABDUL-JABBAR
Master of the Sky-Hook

The gambling town of Las Vegas, Nevada, seemed an unlikely setting for Kareem Abdul-Jabbar on April 5, 1984. The towering Laker center was there for a regular-season NBA game against the Utah Jazz.

In the fourth quarter, Kareem hit on his trademark sky-hook and the sellout crowd of more than 18,000 fans cheered wildly. The 7'2" veteran, in his 15th season, had broken Wilt Chamberlain's all-time NBA regular-season scoring record of 31,149 points.

Kareem would go on to play for five more record-making years before completing a unique and spectacular career at the age of 42. The picture of grace and elegance on the court, Kareem set a harvest of records and bagged awards galore, including six NBA championship rings.

He was inducted into the Basketball Hall of Fame in 1995.

Fantastic Facts About Kareem Abdul-Jabbar

(Born Ferdinand Lewis Alcindor)
Born: April 16, 1947, New York City, New York
Height: 7'2"
Weight: 267

•In his high school basketball career, Kareem led Power Memorial Academy to 71 straight victories. When Kareem played college ball at UCLA, the team had a record of 88-2 and won three NCAA titles.

•Kareem was the No. 1 draft pick in 1969. In his first season with the Milwaukee Bucks he was the NBA's second-leading scorer and was named Rookie of the Year. A year later he led the Bucks to their only NBA championship.

•Kareem is the NBA's all-time leading scorer with 38,387 points. He's also No. 1 in field goals made, field goals attempted, blocked shots, most games played, and most personal fouls.

•He was named NBA MVP 6 times, All-NBA First Team 10 times, NBA All-Defensive Team 5 times, and NBA Finals MVP twice.

Year	Team	G	FG	FG Pct.	FT	FT Pct.	Reb.	Ast.	TP	Avg.
1969-70	Milwaukee	82	938	.518	485	.653	1190	337	2361	28.8
1970-71	Milwaukee	82	1063	.577	470	.690	1311	272	2596	31.7
1971-72	Milwaukee	81	1159	.574	504	.689	1346	370	2822	34.8
1972-73	Milwaukee	76	982	.554	328	.713	1224	379	2292	30.2
1973-74	Milwaukee	81	948	.539	295	.702	1178	386	2191	27.0
1974-75	Milwaukee	65	812	.513	325	.763	912	264	1949	30.0
1975-76	Los Angeles ...	82	914	.529	447	.703	1383	413	2275	27.7
1976-77	Los Angeles ...	82	888	.579	376	.701	1090	319	2152	26.2
1977-78	Los Angeles ...	62	663	.550	274	.783	801	269	1600	25.8
1978-79	Los Angeles ...	80	777	.577	349	.736	1025	431	1903	23.8
1979-80	Los Angeles ...	82	835	.604	364	.765	886	371	2034	24.8
1980-81	Los Angeles ...	80	836	.574	423	.766	821	272	2095	26.2
1981-82	Los Angeles ...	76	753	.579	312	.706	659	225	1818	23.9
1982-83	Los Angeles ...	79	722	.588	278	.749	592	200	1722	21.8
1983-84	Los Angeles ...	80	716	.578	285	.723	587	211	1717	21.5
1984-85	L.A. Lakers	79	723	.599	289	.732	622	249	1735	22.0
1985-86	L.A. Lakers	79	755	.564	336	.765	478	280	1846	23.4
1986-87	L.A. Lakers	78	560	.564	245	.714	523	203	1366	17.5
1987-88	L.A. Lakers	80	480	.532	205	.762	478	135	1165	14.6
1988-89	L.A. Lakers	74	313	.475	122	.739	334	74	748	10.1
	Totals..............	1560	15837	.559	6712	.721	17440	5660	38387	24.6
Playoff Totals..................		237	2356	.533	1050	.740	2481	767	5762	24.3

LARRY BIRD
An All-Around Superstar

As a boy growing up in tiny French Lick, Indiana, Larry Bird didn't own a bike. His mother couldn't afford one. But he and his brothers had a basketball. And almost every day, Larry dribbled the ball up and down the hilly streets to the local playground, where he played from sunrise to sunset.

Nothing else mattered to him but mastery of the game he loved. When he was in high school, his coach "banged the fundamentals" into him over and over. Hour after hour, Bird designed his moves and worked to strengthen his left hand. "I never wanted to leave the court until I got things exactly correct," he said. "My dream was to become a pro."

Larry Bird's dream came true in 1978 when he was selected by the Boston Celtics in the NBA Draft. Almost from the start of his pro career, he became the most complete basketball player to come into the league since Oscar Robertson. He could score, pass, play defense, and lead a team. In 13 seasons, Bird took the Celtics to three NBA championships and, along with Magic Johnson, changed the concept of the game with leadership, unselfishness, competitive spirit, and a flair for the dramatic.

Bird is a certain Hall of Famer when he becomes eligible in 1998.

Fantastic Facts About Larry Bird

Born: December 7, 1956, West Baden, Illinois
Height: 6'9"
Weight: 220

•Bird led Indiana State to the NCAA championship game in 1979, losing to Magic Johnson-led Michigan State. Bird was named College Player of the Year that year.

•The year before the Celtics got Bird they were 29-53, last in the Atlantic Division. In his first year, 1979-80, he led Boston to the NBA's best record, 61-29, and was named Rookie of the Year.

•Bird was named the NBA's MVP in 1984, 1985, and 1986, and he was All-NBA First Team nine straight years, from 1980 to 1988.

•According to Celtics president, Red Auerbach, Bird was "the best passing big man" he'd ever seen. Bird handed out more assists (5,695) than any other forward in the history of the game.

•Bird was a member of the Dream Team that won a gold medal at the 1992 Barcelona Olympics.

Year	Team	G	FG	FG Pct.	FT	FT Pct.	Reb.	Ast.	TP	Avg.
1979-80	Boston	82	693	.474	301	.836	852	370	1745	21.3
1980-81	Boston	82	719	.478	283	.863	895	451	1741	21.2
1981-82	Boston	77	711	.503	328	.863	837	447	1761	22.9
1982-83	Boston	79	747	.504	351	.840	870	458	1867	23.6
1983-84	Boston	79	758	.492	374	.888	796	520	1908	24.2
1984-85	Boston	80	918	.522	403	.882	842	531	2295	28.7
1985-86	Boston	82	796	.496	441	.896	805	557	2115	25.8
1986-87	Boston	74	786	.525	414	.910	682	566	2076	28.1
1987-88	Boston	76	881	.527	415	.916	703	467	2275	29.9
1988-89	Boston	6	49	.471	18	.947	37	29	116	19.3
1989-90	Boston	75	718	.473	319	.930	712	562	1820	24.3
1990-91	Boston	60	462	.454	163	.891	509	431	1164	19.4
1991-92	Boston	45	353	.466	150	.926	434	306	908	20.2
Totals		897	8591	.496	3960	.886	8974	5695	21791	24.3
Playoff Totals		164	1458	.472	901	.890	1683	1062	3897	23.8

WILT CHAMBERLAIN
"The Big Dipper"

When Wilt Chamberlain was a high school senior in Philadelphia in 1955, an article entitled "The High School Kid Who Could Play Pro Right Now" appeared in *Sport* magazine. Wilt was already a 7-footer, and everyone agreed that it was only a matter of time before he would become a towering force in the game.

Four years later everyone found out just what kind of impact Wilt would have on pro basketball. In 1959-60, his first season with the Philadelphia Warriors, "Wilt the Stilt" (later "The Big Dipper") led the NBA in scoring with an awesome 37.6-point average and was named Rookie of the Year.

For the first seven years of his career, Wilt's teams never won a championship. His critics said Wilt selfishly scored points and ignored other aspects of his game that might help his team win. But in 1966-67, Wilt changed his style. He concentrated less on shooting and more on passing. He blocked rivals' shots and went for every rebound. Result: He led the 76ers to the NBA title and was named regular-season MVP. Wilt won a second championship ring with the Los Angeles Lakers in 1972. He retired after the next season, but Wilt left his mark on both the game and the record book.

He was elected to the Basketball Hall of Fame in 1978.

Fantastic Facts About Wilt Chamberlain

Born: August 21, 1936, Philadelphia, Pennsylvania
Height: 7'1"
Weight: 275

•Wilt once grabbed a record 55 rebounds in a game against the Boston Celtics in 1960. He led the NBA in rebounding 11 seasons.

•Wilt is the only player to ever score over 4,000 points in a season. A four-time NBA MVP, he led the NBA in scoring a record seven straight seasons from 1960 to 1966.

•Wilt holds the single-game record for most points, 100, most field goals attempted, 63, most field goals made, 36, and most free throws attempted, 34. He also scored the most points in an All-Star Game, 42. Although Wilt was a 50 percent foul shooter, he still shares the record for most free throws made in a game, 28.

•Wilt never fouled out in 1,205 regular-season and playoff games.

•Wilt made a record 18 consecutive field goals in a 1963 game against the Knicks.

Year	Team	G	FG	FG Pct.	FT	FT Pct.	Reb.	Ast.	TP	Avg.
1959-60	Philadelphia ...	72	1065	.461	577	.582	1941	168	2707	37.6
1960-61	Philadelphia ...	79	1251	.509	531	.504	2149	148	3033	38.4
1961-62	Philadelphia ...	80	1597	.506	835	.613	2052	192	4029	50.4
1962-63	San Francisco.	80	1463	.528	660	.593	1946	275	3586	44.8
1963-64	San Francisco.	80	1204	.524	540	.531	1787	403	2948	36.9
1964-65	S.F.-Phil.	73	1063	.510	408	.464	1673	250	2534	34.7
1965-66	Philadelphia ...	79	1074	.540	501	.513	1943	414	2649	33.5
1966-67	Philadelphia ...	81	785	.683	386	.441	1957	630	1956	24.1
1967-68	Philadelphia ...	82	819	.595	354	.380	1952	702	1992	24.3
1968-69	Los Angeles ...	81	641	.583	382	.446	1712	366	1664	20.5
1969-70	Los Angeles ...	12	129	.568	70	.446	221	49	328	27.3
1970-71	Los Angeles ...	82	668	.545	360	.538	1493	352	1696	20.7
1971-72	Los Angeles ...	82	496	.649	221	.422	1572	329	1213	14.8
1972-73	Los Angeles ...	82	426	.727	232	.510	1526	365	1084	13.2
	Totals..............	1045	12681	.540	6057	.511	23924	4643	31419	30.1
	Playoff Totals..................	160	1425	.522	757	.465	3913	673	3607	22.5

BOB COUSY
Court Magician

Houdini is considered the most famous magician of all time. In basketball, there was no magician to compare with the Boston Celtics' Bob Cousy. He was a ball-handling wizard whose behind-the-back passes and dazzling playmaking inspired sportswriters to label him "Houdini of the Hardwood."

"The Cooz," as he later became known, learned the game on the playgrounds of St. Albans, Queens, a borough of New York City. Later he led Holy Cross to the 1947 NCAA crown. He would go on to play a major role, with Bill Russell, in six Celtics championships. He was such a valuable member of the Celtics squad that when he retired, Boston coach Red Auerbach said, "What can you say when you know you're going to lose the greatest backcourt man who ever lived?"

Cousy was elected to the Basketball Hall of Fame in 1970. Earlier that year, while coaching the Cincinnati Royals, he played seven games at the age of 41.

In 1993, he appeared with Shaq O'Neal and Penny Hardaway in *Blue Chips*. There's a scene in the movie in which Cousy shows he hasn't lost his touch; he makes a batch of consecutive free throws.

Fantastic Facts About Bob Cousy

Born: August 9, 1928, New York City, New York
Height: 6'1"
Weight: 175

• Cousy was the NBA MVP in 1957 and was named to the All-NBA First Team 10 straight years, from 1952 to 1961.

• Cousy played in 13 straight All-Star Games.

• Beginning in 1952-53, Cousy led the NBA in assists eight consecutive years.

• Cousy set a record for most assists in one half in 1959 with 17 against Minneapolis.

• Cousy played seven games for the Cincinnati Royals when he coached the team in 1969-70. He was the oldest performer to play in the league at that time.

Year	Team	G	FG	FG Pct.	FT	FT Pct.	Reb.	Ast.	TP	Avg.
1950-51	Boston	69	401	.352	276	.756	474	341	1078	15.6
1951-52	Boston	66	512	.369	409	.808	421	441	1433	21.7
1952-53	Boston	71	464	.352	479	.816	449	547	1407	19.8
1953-54	Boston	72	486	.385	411	.787	394	518	1383	19.2
1954-55	Boston	71	522	.397	460	.807	424	557	1504	21.2
1955-56	Boston	72	440	.360	476	.844	492	642	1356	18.8
1956-57	Boston	64	478	.378	363	.821	309	478	1319	20.6
1957-58	Boston	65	445	.353	277	.850	322	463	1167	18.0
1958-59	Boston	65	484	.384	329	.855	359	557	1297	20.0
1959-60	Boston	75	568	.384	319	.792	352	715	1455	19.4
1960-61	Boston	76	513	.371	352	.779	331	591	1378	18.1
1961-62	Boston	75	462	.391	251	.754	261	584	1175	15.7
1962-63	Boston	76	392	.397	219	.735	201	515	1003	13.2
1969-70	Cincinnati	7	1	.333	3	1.000	5	10	5	0.7
Totals		924	6168	.375	4624	.803	4794	6959	16960	18.4
Playoff Totals		109	689	.342	640	.801	546	937	2018	18.5

JULIUS ERVING
"Dr. J"

He was a superstar, but he seemed superhuman. He stood 6'6", 220 pounds, but his shoulders and arms bordered on massive. His legs were sleek and powerful, his hands positively enormous. But what really set Julius Winfield Erving, Jr. apart from all other basketball players in the 1970s were his above-the-hoop flights and show-stopping moves. He created new standards for excellence and excitement in pro basketball. Erving captivated fans by doing things that had never been seen before. His twirling dunks and acrobatic moves became the stuff of legend.

As a high school basketball star Erving was fearless and flamboyant, trying to do trickery with the ball while scoring at the same time. When he got the nickname "Dr. J," many thought it was because of his precise and delicate moves. But Erving said it really derived from a friend after Julius told him he was going to be a doctor.

He began his pro career in 1971 with the Virginia Squires in the ABA (American Basketball Association). Virginia sold him to the New Jersey Nets in 1973 and he promptly led them to the ABA title. Later, after the ABA merged with the NBA, he joined the Philadelphia 76ers and became a Philadelphia folk hero—for his on-court exploits and his grace and eloquence off-court. Today, Dr. J remains an ambassador for the game of basketball and a hero to many of today's NBA stars.

He was inducted into the Basketball Hall of Fame in 1993.

Fantastic Facts About Julius Erving

Born: February 22, 1950, Roosevelt, New York
Height: 6'6"
Weight: 220

•Erving not only led the Nets to two ABA titles, he also led the 76ers to the NBA title in 1983.

•Dr. J was a three-time ABA MVP and a one-time NBA MVP.

•In both 1977 and 1983 Erving was the All-Star Game MVP.

•During his college career, Erving became one of a select group of players to average 20 points and 20 rebounds per game.

•In his combined ABA-NBA career, Erving scored more than 30,000 points.

Year	Team	G	FG	FG Pct.	FT	FT Pct.	Reb.	Ast.	TP	Avg.
1971-72	Virginia (ABA) ..	84	910	.498	467	.745	1319	335	2290	27.3
1972-73	Virginia (ABA) ..	71	894	.496	475	.776	867	298	2268	31.9
1973-74	New York (ABA)	84	914	.512	454	.766	899	434	2299	27.4
1974-75	New York (ABA)	84	914	.506	486	.799	914	462	2343	27.9
1975-76	New York (ABA)	84	949	.507	530	.801	925	423	2462	29.3
1976-77	Philadelphia ...	82	685	.499	400	.777	695	306	1770	21.6
1977-78	Philadelphia ...	74	611	.502	306	.845	481	279	1528	20.6
1978-79	Philadelphia ...	78	715	.491	373	.745	564	357	1803	23.1
1979-80	Philadelphia ...	78	838	.519	420	.787	576	355	2100	26.9
1980-81	Philadelphia ...	82	794	.521	422	.787	657	364	2014	24.6
1981-82	Philadelphia ...	81	780	.546	411	.763	557	319	1974	24.4
1982-83	Philadelphia ...	72	605	.517	330	.759	491	263	1542	21.4
1983-84	Philadelphia ...	77	678	.512	364	.754	532	309	1727	22.4
1984-85	Philadelphia ...	78	610	.494	338	.765	414	233	1561	20.0
1985-86	Philadelphia ...	74	521	.480	289	.785	370	248	1340	18.1
1986-87	Philadelphia ...	60	400	.471	191	.813	264	191	1005	16.8
	NBA Totals......	836	7237	.507	3844	.777	5601	3224	18364	22.0
	ABA Totals......	407	4581	.504	2412	.778	4924	1952	11662	28.7
NBA Playoff Totals...........		141	1187	.486	707	.779	994	594	3088	21.9
ABA Playoff Totals...........		48	582	.519	318	.795	617	247	1492	31.1

MAGIC JOHNSON
"Showtime"

When he was at Everett High School in Lansing, Michigan, a local sportswriter called him "Magic." Magic because of his effervescent smile. Magic because he was such a talented basketball player. But mostly he was Magic because he somehow transformed good teams into great teams. Earvin Johnson did that everywhere he went—in high school, at Michigan State, and then with the Los Angeles Lakers.

The No. 1 pick overall in the 1979 Draft, Magic turned on the Lakers and the league immediately with his joyful exuberance. Magic quickly introduced "Showtime" and "Winnin' Time" to the Hollywood crowd. And fittingly, the ending to his remarkable rookie year was pure Hollywood. After leading the Lakers through the playoffs, Magic started at center in place of the injured Kareem Abdul-Jabbar in the decisive Game 6 of the 1980 NBA Finals against Philadelphia. He finished with 42 points, 15 rebounds, and 7 assists in one of the greatest playoff efforts of all time, giving the Lakers the NBA crown. He was the Finals MVP and named to the All-Rookie team.

With Magic at the point—"a coach on the floor," his former coach Pat Riley called him—the Lakers won five championships in the 1980s.

Magic retired in 1991 after announcing that he had contracted the virus that causes AIDS. In 1994, he coached the Lakers for a stint, before becoming part-owner of the team he served so magically on the court.

He remains active, playing with a team called Magic

Johnson's All-Stars that tours all over the world.

Magic is a shoo-in for the Basketball Hall of Fame when he becomes eligible for election in 1997.

Fantastic Facts About Magic Johnson

Born: August 14, 1959, Lansing, Michigan
Height: 6'9"
Weight: 220

•In 1977 Magic led his Everett High School team to a 27-1 record and the state championship. Two years later, he helped Michigan State win the NCAA title.

•Magic was the NBA's regular season MVP three times, Playoff MVP three times, and All-Star Game MVP once.

•Magic was named to the All-NBA First Team nine times.

•As a member of the 1992 Dream Team, Magic won a gold medal at the Barcelona Olympics.

•Magic and Larry Bird engaged in legendary duels throughout their NBA careers. In Bird's opinion, "Magic is the best basketball player I've ever seen."

Year	Team	G	FG	FG Pct.	FT	FT Pct.	Reb.	Ast.	TP	Avg.
1979-80	Los Angeles ...77		503	.530	374	.810	596	563	1387	18.0
1980-81	Los Angeles ...37		312	.532	171	.760	320	317	798	21.6
1981-82	Los Angeles ...78		556	.537	329	.760	751	743	1447	18.6
1982-83	Los Angeles ...79		511	.548	304	.800	683	829	1326	16.8
1983-84	Los Angeles ...67		441	.565	290	.810	491	875	1178	17.6
1984-85	Los Angeles ...77		504	.561	391	.843	476	968	1406	18.3
1985-86	Los Angeles ...72		483	.526	378	.871	426	907	1354	18.8
1986-87	Los Angeles ...80		683	.522	535	.848	504	977	1909	23.9
1987-88	Los Angeles ...72		490	.492	417	.853	449	858	1408	19.6
1988-89	Los Angeles ...77		579	.509	513	.911	607	988	1730	22.5
1989-90	Los Angeles ...79		546	.480	567	.890	522	907	1765	22.3
1990-91	Los Angeles ...79		466	.477	519	.906	551	989	1531	19.4
	Totals 874		6074	.521	4788	.848	6376	9921	17239	19.7
Playoff Totals 186			1276	.508	1040	.838	1431	2320	3640	19.6

OSCAR ROBERTSON
"The Big O"

For youngsters and oldsters alike, Oscar Robertson held a clinic in basketball technique every time he stepped onto the court. All you needed was a ticket to the game. Then you watched his every move.

No guard shot better. No guard rebounded better. No guard excelled so consistently as the player known as "The Big O." In a marvelous 14-year NBA career, Robertson set new standards for guard play.

A scoring star in both high school and college, Robertson was a key member of the 1960 U.S. Olympic team that won a gold medal in Rome. That same year he joined the Cincinnati Royals. He had played forward exclusively as a collegian, but switched to guard as a pro and was Rookie of the Year in 1961, averaging 30.5 points and 9.7 assists, setting a playmaking record he would exceed many times.

Despite Robertson's enormous presence over a 10-year period, the Royals never won a championship. But Robertson did, after being traded to the Milwaukee Bucks in 1970. Robertson was 32 by then, and the Bucks were being built around a young center named Kareem Abdul-Jabbar. Robertson gave the Bucks just the sort of leadership and inspiration they needed. And they won the title in 1970-71.

"The Big O" was inducted into the Basketball Hall of Fame in 1980.

Fantastic Facts About Oscar Robertson

Born: November 24, 1938, Charlotte, Tennessee
Height: 6'5"
Weight: 205

•Robertson led his high school team to 45 straight victories and two straight state championships. At the University of Cincinnati, Robertson led the nation in scoring and was College Player of the Year all three seasons he played.

•In 1961-62, his second season, Robertson achieved something no other player has done by averaging a triple-double for the entire season—30.8 points, 12.5 rebounds, and 11.4 assists per game.

•The Big O was named to the All-NBA First Team nine times.

•He was the NBA MVP in 1964 and All-Star Game MVP three times.

•Robertson led the NBA in assists six times.

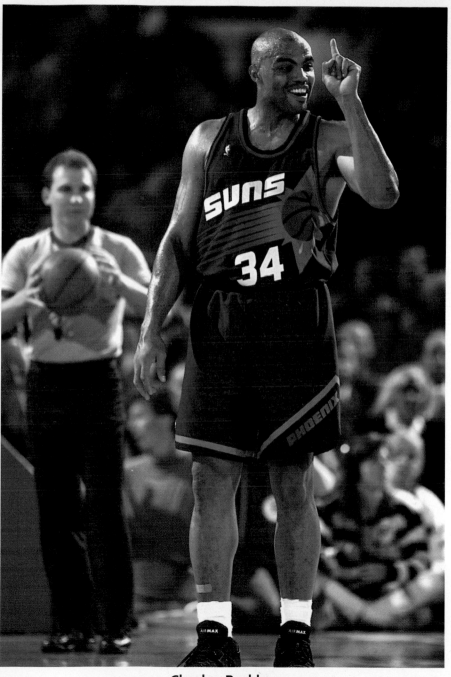

Charles Barkley

Karl Malone and David Robinson

Michael Jordan

Grant Hill

Alonzo Mourning (now with Miami)

Jason Kidd

Muggsy Bogues

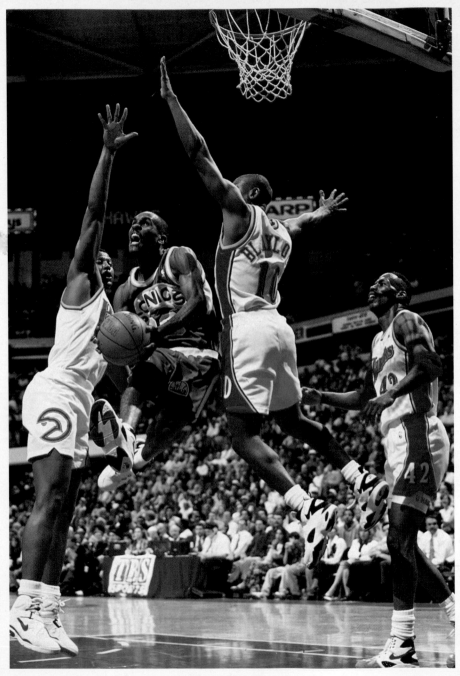

Gary Payton

Year	Team	G	FG	FG Pct.	FT	FT Pct.	Reb.	Ast.	TP	Avg.
1960-61	Cincinnati.......	71	756	.473	653	.822	716	690	2165	30.5
1961-62	Cincinnati.......	79	866	.478	700	.803	985	899	2432	30.8
1962-63	Cincinnati.......	80	825	.518	614	.810	835	758	2264	28.3
1963-64	Cincinnati.......	79	840	.483	800	.853	783	868	2480	31.4
1964-65	Cincinnati.......	75	807	.480	665	.839	674	861	2279	30.4
1965-66	Cincinnati.......	76	818	.475	742	.842	586	847	2378	31.3
1966-67	Cincinnati.......	79	838	.493	736	.873	486	845	2412	30.5
1967-68	Cincinnati.......	65	660	.500	576	.873	391	633	1896	29.2
1968-69	Cincinnati.......	79	656	.486	643	.838	502	772	1955	24.7
1969-70	Cincinnati.......	69	647	.511	454	.809	422	558	1748	25.3
1970-71	Milwaukee.....	81	592	.496	385	.850	462	668	1569	19.4
1971-72	Milwaukee.....	64	419	.472	276	.836	323	491	1114	17.4
1972-73	Milwaukee.....	73	446	.454	238	.847	360	551	1130	15.5
1973-74	Milwaukee.....	70	338	.438	212	.835	279	446	888	12.7
	Totals..............	1040	9508	.485	7694	.838	7804	9887	26710	25.7
	Playoff Totals..................	86	675	.460	560	.855	578	769	1910	22.2

BILL RUSSELL
Dean of Defense

From 1957 to 1969 the Boston Celtics were a dynasty that won 11 NBA titles, 8 of them in a row. One of the biggest reasons for the Celtics' success was their sensational center Bill Russell.

Selected third overall by the Boston Celtics in the 1956 NBA Draft, he introduced rebounding and shot-blocking as new art forms in the pro game. Russell's awesome catlike movements and tremendous timing intimidated countless shooters. His mobility helped redefine the center position. His unique skills made him the greatest defensive player in NBA history.

"He was the ultimate team player," Hall-of-Fame Celtic Bob Cousy said. "Without Bill there would have been no Celtic dynasty."

Or fabled Celtic fast break. It was Russell's mastery of the boards that got the ball in the hands of his fast-breaking teammates. He developed a sound hook shot and good baseline shot, and he glorified the blocked shot.

In 1966, he became Boston's player-coach, the first black coach in NBA history. He led the Celtics to two titles in three years as coach before retiring from both positions in 1969, at the age of 35. He was elected to the Basketball Hall of Fame five years later.

Fantastic Facts About Bill Russell

Born: February 12, 1934, Monroe, Louisiana
Height: 6'10"
Weight: 220

•Russell was the NBA MVP five times and an All-NBA First Team selection three times.

•In a 1957 game against Philadelphia, Russell grabbed 32 rebounds in one half, setting an NBA record. He led the NBA in rebounding four seasons, and in his 13-year career averaged an amazing 22.5 rebounds per game.

•He won a gold medal [with the U.S. team] at the 1956 Olympic Games in Melbourne, Australia.

•He was named to the NBA 25th and 35th Anniversary All-Time Teams in 1970 and 1980.

•Russell was selected as "the Greatest Player in the History of the NBA" by the Professional Basketball Writers Association of America in 1980.

Year	Team	G	FG	FG Pct.	FT	FT Pct.	Reb.	Ast.	TP	Avg.
1956-57	Boston	48	277	.427	152	.492	943	88	706	14.7
1957-58	Boston	69	456	.442	230	.519	1564	202	1142	16.6
1958-59	Boston	70	456	.457	256	.598	1612	222	1168	16.7
1959-60	Boston	74	555	.467	240	.612	1778	277	1350	18.2
1960-61	Boston	78	532	.426	258	.550	1868	264	1322	16.9
1961-62	Boston	76	575	.457	286	.595	1891	341	1436	18.9
1962-63	Boston	78	511	.432	287	.555	1843	348	1309	16.8
1963-64	Boston	78	466	.433	236	.550	1930	370	1168	15.0
1964-65	Boston	78	429	.438	244	.573	1878	410	1102	14.1
1965-66	Boston	78	391	.415	223	.551	1779	371	1005	12.9
1966-67	Boston	81	395	.454	285	.610	1700	472	1075	13.3
1967-68	Boston	78	365	.425	247	.537	1451	357	977	12.5
1968-69	Boston	77	279	.433	204	.526	1484	374	762	9.9
Totals		963	5687	.440	3148	.561	21721	4096	14522	15.1
Playoff Totals		165	1003	.430	667	.603	4104	770	2673	16.2

ISIAH THOMAS
Zig-Zagging with "Zeke"

He was the youngest of Mary Thomas' nine children, growing up in a Chicago ghetto surrounded by drugs and street gangs. But Isiah Lord Thomas managed to avoid getting caught in the net of that troubled world. Instead, he found escape in basketball.

And basketball never saw a more dominant "little man" than Isiah Thomas. A free-spirited point guard with an engaging smile, Thomas was a dazzling passer, fearless penetrator, and one of the game's great clutch shooters, as well as a born leader.

The Detroit Pistons chose him No. 2 out of Indiana in the 1981 Draft. He became the team leader on and off the court, bringing together a mix of personalities known as the "Bad Boys" for their aggressive play. Thomas ultimately took the team to back-to-back titles in 1989 and 1990.

He was equally deft with the 3-point shot as he was scoring in traffic, often outmaneuvering 7-footers. Thomas was respected as one of a handful of players in the 1980s—along with Larry Bird, Michael Jordan, and Magic Johnson—who could almost single-handedly take over a game.

"He had a lot of heart," said former teammate Vinnie Johnson. "Whatever the team needed, 'Zeke' provided it. He showed that with sacrifice, you could win."

After retiring as a player in 1994, Isiah became vice president of the expansion Toronto Raptors.

Fantastic Facts About Isiah Thomas

Born: April 30, 1961, Chicago, Illinois
Height: 6'1"
Weight: 185

•Thomas is the Detroit Pistons' all-time leader in points, assists, and steals. He led the NBA in assists in 1985.

•Thomas was the MVP in the NBA Finals in 1990 and All-Star Game MVP twice.

•He was named to the All-NBA First Team three times.

•In a playoff game against the Lakers in 1988, Thomas set an NBA record by scoring 25 points in a quarter.

•He was a member of the 1980 U.S. Olympic Team.

Year	Team	G	FG	FG Pct.	FT	FT Pct.	Reb.	Ast.	TP	Avg.
1981-82	Detroit............	72	453	.424	302	.704	209	565	1225	17.0
1982-83	Detroit............	81	725	.472	368	.710	328	634	1854	22.9
1983-84	Detroit............	82	669	.462	388	.733	327	914	1748	21.3
1984-85	Detroit............	81	646	.458	399	.809	361	1123	1720	21.2
1985-86	Detroit............	77	609	.488	365	.790	277	830	1609	20.9
1986-87	Detroit............	81	626	.463	400	.768	319	813	1671	20.6
1987-88	Detroit............	81	621	.463	305	.774	278	678	1577	19.5
1988-89	Detroit............	80	569	.464	287	.818	273	663	1458	18.2
1989-90	Detroit............	81	579	.438	292	.775	308	765	1492	18.4
1990-91	Detroit............	48	289	.435	179	.782	160	446	776	16.2
1991-92	Detroit............	78	564	.446	292	.772	247	560	1445	18.5
1992-93	Detroit............	79	526	.418	278	.737	232	671	1391	17.6
1993-94	Detroit............	58	318	.417	181	.702	159	399	856	14.8
	Totals..............	979	7194	.452	4036	.759	3478	9061	18822	19.2
Playoff Totals.................		111	825	.441	530	.769	524	987	2261	20.4

JERRY WEST
"Mr. Clutch"

Like most great players, Jerry West was superb under pressure. "I learned," he once said, "that no matter what happens in a game, the last four minutes seem to decide it. So when it comes, I'm ready."

So ready was he on so many occasions that he earned the nickname "Mr. Clutch." Nobody could deny that description, for he won countless regular-season games, playoff games, and the 1972 All-Star Game with clutch shots.

In the 1969 NBA Finals, West's Los Angeles Lakers were battling the Boston Celtics for the sixth time in eight seasons. The previous five series had ended in defeat for Los Angeles. And now it came down to Game 7. But the Celtics won again, despite West's 42 points, 13 rebounds, and 12 assists.

Celtic captain John Havlicek put his arm around Jerry and told him how much the team respected him and how they hoped one day he would win a championship. He and the Lakers finally did—in the 1971-72 season in which Los Angeles had an incredible 33-game winning streak.

West was inducted into the Basketball Hall of Fame in 1979. He now serves the Lakers as executive vice president.

Fantastic Facts About Jerry West

Born: May 28, 1938, Cheylan, West Virginia
Height: 6'3"
Weight: 175

•When West retired after the 1973-74 season he was the third-leading scorer in NBA history with 25,192 points. He had averaged 27 points per game. In a remarkable game against the Knicks, West poured in 63 points.

•West was a member of the U.S. Olympic team that won the gold medal in Rome in 1960.

•He was an All-NBA First Team selection 10 times and NBA All-Defensive First Team four straight seasons (1970-73).

•Mr. Clutch was the Playoff MVP in 1969 and All-Star Game MVP in 1972.

•In 1965-66 West made 840 free throws, setting an NBA one-season record.

Year	Team	G	FG	FG Pct.	FT	FT Pct.	Reb.	Ast.	TP	Avg.
1960-61	Los Angeles ...	79	529	.419	331	.666	611	333	1389	17.6
1961-62	Los Angeles ...	75	799	.445	712	.769	591	402	2310	30.8
1962-63	Los Angeles ...	55	559	.461	371	.778	384	307	1489	27.1
1963-64	Los Angeles ...	72	740	.484	584	.832	443	403	2064	28.7
1964-65	Los Angeles ...	74	822	.497	648	.821	447	364	2292	31.0
1965-66	Los Angeles ...	79	818	.473	840	.860	562	480	2476	31.3
1966-67	Los Angeles ...	66	645	.464	602	.878	392	447	1892	28.7
1967-68	Los Angeles ...	51	476	.514	391	.811	294	310	1343	26.3
1968-69	Los Angeles ...	61	545	.471	490	.821	262	423	1580	25.9
1969-70	Los Angeles ...	74	831	.497	647	.824	338	554	2309	31.2
1970-71	Los Angeles ...	69	667	.494	525	.832	320	655	1859	26.9
1971-72	Los Angeles ...	77	735	.477	515	.814	327	747	1985	25.8
1972-73	Los Angeles ...	69	618	.479	339	.805	289	607	1575	22.8
1973-74	Los Angeles ...	31	232	.447	165	.833	116	206	629	20.3
Totals..............		932	9016	.474	7160	.814	5376	6238	25192	27.0
Playoff Totals..................		153	1622	.469	1213	.805	855	970	4457	29.1

Let's Go to the Movies

— — —

You're a basketball addict. It's raining. No shooting hoops today. No NBA game on television. What to do? Well, how about a basketball movie? Here is a list of basketball movies, many of them available at your local video store:

Above the Rim (1993): Drama about a high school basketball star trying to escape life on the mean streets and deciding to pursue a career as a ballplayer.

Blue Chips (1993): Drama about a college basketball coach (Nick Nolte) who finds himself having to break the rules in his search for players. Also with Shaquille O'Neal, Larry Bird, Bob Cousy, Anfernee Hardaway, Bobby Knight, Bobby Hurley, and Rick Pitino.

Drive, He Said (1972): A gung-ho college basketball coach (Bruce Dern) tries to solve some of his players' off-the-court problems. This was Jack Nicholson's first movie as a director.

Fast Break (1979): A comedy about a basketball coach (Gabriel Kaplan) who brings his street-smart New York City players to his new team as coach of a midwestern college.

Final Shot—The Hank Gathers Story (1993): The true story of a young basketball player (played by Victor Love) who escaped the ghetto to become a star at Loyola Marymount College. He was destined for a big career in the NBA, but then tragedy struck.

Forget Paris (1995): A romantic comedy featuring Billy Crystal as an NBA referee and Debra Winger. The film captures the excitement of basketball and has a cast of NBA players, including Charles Barkley and David Robinson.

Go, Man, Go (1954): How the Harlem Globetrotters were formed and became basketball's most magical team.

Hoop Dreams (1994): A documentary that follows the ups and downs of two young basketball players from urban Chicago. The film, shot over a seven-year period, begins with the boys at age 14 and deals with dreams of making it in the pros, pressure to succeed, and how their education is affected by the process.

Hoosiers (1986): Down on his luck, a coach (Gene Hackman) gets a last-chance job with a small-town Indiana high school team. He faces the dual challenge of winning the state championship and redeeming himself.

Maurie (1973): The touching story of how NBA star Maurice Stokes (Bernie Casey) suffers a paralyzing illness and receives care and devotion from his teammate Jack Twyman (Bo Svenson).

One on One (1977): An innocent basketball player (Robby Benson) rebels against the evils of big-time college basketball and a sadistic coach.

That Championship Season (1982): A fatherly high school coach (Robert Mitchum) has a 24th reunion with his championship team and they discover all was not as it seemed.

The Air Up There (1994): A comedy about a struggling American basketball coach (Kevin Bacon) who wants to recruit a talented young African.

The Fish That Saved Pittsburgh (1979): A comedy about a losing basketball team that tries to use astrology to get into the winner's circle. With Julius Erving, Jonathan Winters, Meadowlark Lemon, Flip Wilson, Kareem Abdul-Jabbar, and Marv Albert.

All-Star Weekend

It all started simply as an All-Star Game in 1951, pitting the best players of the East against the best of the West. But in 1984 it became more than a game. They called it All-Star Weekend, adding a Slam-Dunk Championship in 1984 for the NBA's super-dunkers. In 1986, a long-distance shootout for the deadliest 3-point players was a new attraction, along with a Legends game, which began in 1984, and was replaced in 1994 by a game for rookies only.

The Lakers' Cedric Ceballos electrified the fans with a memorable feat in the 1992 Slam-Dunk Championship in Orlando. Wearing a black blindfold on his last jump, he raced three-quarters of the length of the floor and slammed the ball home. He'd already won the event when he tried the shot that capped a perfect score and brought him the $20,000 first prize.

Bob Pettit holds the record for most MVP awards (4) in an All-Star Game.

All-Star Game Results

Year	Result	Location	Most Valuable Player
1951	East 111, West 94	Boston	Ed Macauley, Boston
1952	East 108, West 91	Boston	Paul Arizin, Philadelphia
1953	West 79, East 75	Fort Wayne	George Mikan, Minneapolis
1954	East 98, West 93 (OT)	New York	Bob Cousy, Boston

1995	East 100, West 91	New York	Bill Sharman, Boston
1956	West 108, East 94	Rochester	Bob Pettit, St. Louis
1957	East 109, West 97	Boston	Bob Cousy, Boston
1958	East 130, West 118	St. Louis	Bob Pettit, St. Louis
1959	West 124, East 108	Detroit	Elgin Baylor, Minneapolis Bob Pettit, St. Louis
1960	East 125, West 115	Philadelphia	Wilt Chamberlain, Philadelphia
1961	West 153, East 131	Syracuse	Oscar Robertson, Cincinnati
1962	West 150, East 130	St. Louis	Bob Pettit, St. Louis
1963	East 115, West 108	Los Angeles	Bill Russell, Boston
1964	East 111, West 107	Boston	Oscar Robertson, Cincinnati
1965	East 124, West 123	St. Louis	Jerry Lucas, Cincinnati
1966	East 127, West 94	Cincinnati	Adrian Smith, Cincinnati
1967	West 135, East 120	San Francisco	Rick Barry, San Francisco
1968	East 144, West 124	New York	Hal Greer, Philadelphia
1969	East 123, West 112	Baltimore	Oscar Robertson, Cincinnati
1970	East 142, West 135	Philadelphia	Willis Reed, New York
1971	West 108, East 107	San Diego	Lenny Wilkens, Seattle
1972	West 112, East 110	Los Angeles	Jerry West, Los Angeles
1973	East 104, West 84	Chicago	Dave Cowens, Boston
1974	West 134, East 123	Seattle	Bob Lanier, Detroit
1975	East 108, West 102	Phoenix	Walt Frazier, New York
1976	East 123, West 109	Philadelphia	Dave Bing, Washington
1977	West 125, East 124	Milwaukee	Julius Erving, Philadelphia
1978	East 133, West 125	Atlanta	Randy Smith, Buffalo
1979	West 134, East 129	Detroit	David Thompson, Denver
1980	East 144, West 135 (OT) Washington		George Gervin, San Antonio
1981	East 123, West 120	Cleveland	Nate Archibald, Boston

Year	Score	Host	MVP
1982	East 120, West 118	New Jersey	Larry Bird, Boston
1983	East 132, West 123	Los Angeles	Julius Erving, Philadelphia
1984	East 154, West 145 (OT)	Denver	Isiah Thomas, Detroit
1985	West 140, East 129	Indianapolis	Ralph Sampson, Houston
1986	East 139, West 132	Dallas	Isiah Thomas, Detroit
1987	West 154, East 149 (OT)	Seattle	Tom Chambers, Seattle
1988	East 138, West 133	Chicago	Michael Jordan, Chicago
1989	West 143, East 134	Houston	Karl Malone, Utah
1990	East 130, West 113	Miami	Magic Johnson, L.A. Lakers
1991	East 116, West 114	Charlotte	Charles Barkley, Philadelphia
1992	West 153, East 113	Orlando	Magic Johnson, L.A. Lakers
1993	West 135, East 132 (OT)	Utah	Karl Malone, Utah John Stockton, Utah
1994	East 127, West 118	Minneapolis	Scottie Pippen, Chicago
1995	West 139, East 112	Phoenix	Mitch Richmond, Sacramento

AT&T Long Distance Shootout		Nestle Crunch Slam-Dunk	
Year	Winner	Year	Winner
1986	Larry Bird	1984	Larry Nance
1987	Larry Bird	1985	Dominique Wilkins
1988	Larry Bird	1986	Spud Webb
1989	Dale Ellis	1987	Michael Jordan
1990	Craig Hodges	1988	Michael Jordan
1991	Craig Hodges	1989	Kenny Walker
1992	Craig Hodges	1990	Dominique Wilkins
1993	Mark Price	1991	Dee Brown
1994	Mark Price	1992	Cedric Ceballos
1995	Glen Rice	1993	Harold Miner
		1994	Isaiah Rider
		1995	Harold Miner

The Draft

The best college players are chosen by the NBA teams through an annual draft. It provides a chance for the weaker teams to improve themselves. For many years, the team with the worst record in the league would draft first. Then came a change in which the teams with the two worst records would flip a coin to determine who would pick first.

In 1985 the NBA altered the method by having the teams that did not make the playoffs entered in a luck-of-the-draw lottery. That was the year the New York Knicks won the rights to the No. 1 pick, which they used to select Georgetown's Patrick Ewing.

The 1995 lottery was won by the Golden State Warriors, who chose Maryland's Joe Smith.

Though the draft started in 1947, records are incomplete until 1957. A listing of the No. 1 players taken in the draft follows:

Year	Player, College	Taken By
1957	Rod Hundley, West Virginia	Cincinnati
1958	Elgin Baylor, Seattle	Minneapolis
1959	Bob Boozer, Kansas State	Cincinnati
1960	Oscar Robertson, Cincinnati	Cincinnati
1961	Walt Bellamy, Indiana	Chicago
1962	Bill McGill, Utah	Chicago
1963	Art Heyman, Duke	New York

1964	Jim Barnes, Texas Western	New York
1965	Fred Hetzel, Davidson	San Francisco
1966	Cazzie Russell, Michigan	New York
1967	Jimmy Walker, Providence	Detroit
1968	Elvin Hayes, Houston	San Diego
1969	Kareem Abdul-Jabbar, UCLA	Milwaukee
1970	Bob Lanier, St. Bonaventure	Detroit
1971	Austin Carr, Notre Dame	Cleveland
1972	LaRue Martin, Loyola (Illinois)	Portland
1973	Doug Collins, Illinois State	Philadelphia
1974	Bill Walton, UCLA	Portland
1975	David Thompson, N. C. State	Atlanta
1976	John Lucas, Maryland	Houston
1977	Kent Benson, Indiana	Milwaukee
1978	Mychal Thompson, Minnesota	Portland
1979	Earvin Johnson, Michigan State	L.A. Lakers
1980	Joe Barry Carroll, Purdue	Golden State
1981	Mark Aguirre, DePaul	Dallas
1982	James Worthy, North Carolina	L.A. Lakers
1983	Ralph Sampson, Virginia	Houston
1984	Hakeem Olajuwon, Houston	Houston
1985	Patrick Ewing, Georgetown	New York
1986	Brad Daugherty, North Carolina	Cleveland
1987	David Robinson, Navy	San Antonio
1988	Danny Manning, Kansas	L.A. Clippers
1989	Pervis Ellison, Louisville	Sacramento
1990	Derrick Coleman, Syracuse	New Jersey
1991	Larry Johnson, Nevada-Las Vegas	Charlotte
1992	Shaquille O'Neal, Louisiana State	Orlando
1993	Chris Webber, Michigan	Orlando
1994	Glenn Robinson, Purdue	Milwaukee
1995	Joe Smith, Maryland	Golden State

Your Favorite Team

— — —

You live in San Francisco, but you root for the San Antonio Spurs because you were born there. Your dad took you to a Celtics game when you were eight and you've been hooked ever since. You're from Vancouver and now you've got the Grizzlies to follow.

Whatever your team, there's one for everyone—well, 29 NBA teams—and you can look 'em up in the mini-histories that follow.

The Atlanta Hawks have come a long way in their illustrious history in the NBA. The team entered the league in 1949-50, when it was called the Tri-Cities Blackhawks and played its games in Iowa and Illinois. After two seasons there, the club moved to Milwaukee and shortened its nickname to Hawks. The team found its greatest success after moving to St. Louis in 1955.

For the next few seasons the Hawks were the Boston Celtics' main challengers for the NBA championship. Starting in 1957, St. Louis won five straight Western Conference titles. The Hawks advanced to the NBA Finals four times, and in 1958 won the only championship in club history by defeating the Celtics in six games in the Finals. The stars of the team were Bob Pettit, who scored 50 points in the clinching game, Cliff Hagan, Clyde Lovellette, and Slater Martin.

The Hawks enjoyed some degree of success through the early 1960s, reaching the Finals in 1960 and 1961, only to lose to the Celtics each time. The prospect of a new building in Atlanta prompted the team to move there in 1968, and the Hawks gave their new fans plenty to cheer about with stars like Lou Hudson and Pete Maravich providing thrills night after night.

Though they did not win a championship, the 1986-87 Hawks were perhaps the best team in club history. Led by dynamic Dominique Wilkins and 7-footer Kevin Willis, the Hawks finished with a record of 57-25 for first place in the Central Division. Wilkins averaged 29.0 points, second in the league behind Michael Jordan.

But the Hawks, even with homecourt advantage, could not bring a title to Atlanta. They lost to the Detroit Pistons, 4-1, in the Eastern Conference semifinals.

Over the next few seasons the scoring of Wilkins and the leadership of Glenn "Doc" Rivers kept the Hawks close to the top of the Central Division, but it wasn't until 1993-94, when former Hawk star Lenny Wilkens took over as coach, that the club showed signs of becoming a championship contender. Dominique Wilkins was traded to the Los Angeles Clippers for Danny Manning, who combined with Willis (now with Miami), Stacey Augmon, and Mookie Blaylock to help the Hawks win the Central Division with a 57-25 record. (Willis was traded to Miami in 1994 in a deal that brought Steve Smith to the Hawks, and Manning is now with Phoenix.)

The Hawks slipped to 42-40 in 1994-95 but again earned a playoff berth. The highlight of the year was Wilkens earning his 939th victory, passing Red Auerbach to become the league's all-time winningest coach. The addition of rookie Alan Henderson, Indiana University's all-time leader in blocks and rebounds, gave Wilkens one more weapon to work with in 1995-96.

Bob Cousy. Bill Russell. John Havlicek. Dave Cowens. Larry Bird. With players like these, it's easy to see why the Boston Celtics are by far the most successful club in the history of professional basketball.

As a charter member of the Basketball Association of America in 1946, the Celtics struggled through some lean times in their early years. They had losing records in each of their first four seasons and failed to make the playoffs in three of those years.

Then Arnold "Red" Auerbach took over as coach, and things turned around immediately. Auerbach guided the Celtics to a 16½-game improvement (22-46 to 39-30). The arrival of rookie guard Bob Cousy in 1951 made the Celtics contenders, and the acquisition of shot-blocking wizard Bill Russell in 1956 made them champions.

Russell's arrival changed the NBA game as defense and shot-blocking became keys to winning. The Celtics won the NBA title in 1956-57, Russell's rookie year, by outlasting the St. Louis Hawks, 125-123, in double overtime of Game 7 at Boston Garden. They lost the title to the Hawks the following year when Russell hurt his ankle in the Finals, but then won again in 1958, starting an incredible run of eight consecutive championships.

The Celtics of Russell, Cousy, Tommy Heinsohn, Satch Sanders, and Sam and K.C. Jones dominated the league through the first half of the 1960s. And when they needed help, Auerbach traded well (picking up Don Nelson) and drafted Havlicek.

Auerbach handed over the coaching reins to Russell in 1966, and the Celtics' streak of titles was ended by the Philadelphia 76ers. But Boston regrouped and won two more titles (1968, 1969). Heinsohn took over for Russell after the second title and, with Dave Cowens in the middle, led the team to championships in 1974 and 1976.

The Celtics, with a corps of All-Stars in Bird, Kevin McHale, Robert Parish, and Dennis Johnson, went on to win three more championships in the 1980s. That gave them 16 titles, five more than their closest franchise competitor, the Lakers (Minneapolis, Los Angeles).

The Celtics were devastated by tragedy in the late 1980s and early 1990s. Len Bias, expected by many to become an NBA star, died immediately after the Celtics drafted him, and then Reggie Lewis, who was on his way to superstardom, died of heart problems. Still, the play of former European star Dino Radja and center Eric Montross, plus the return of hometown hero Dana Barros, gave the Celtics some hope as the 1995-96 season began.

Bzzzz. That's the sound that blares over the public-address system at the Charlotte Coliseum when opponents have the ball. Not that the Coliseum needs any more sound; the hometown Charlotte Hornets have given the fans much to yell about in a very short time.

The Hornets entered the league in 1988-89, joining the Miami Heat as expansion teams. The fans in Charlotte, who follow college basketball with a passion, fell in love with their new team immediately, but that enthusiasm did not translate into many wins on the court at first.

Led by Kelly Tripucka, mighty mite Muggsy Bogues, Dell Curry, and Rex Chapman, the Hornets entertained their fans with fast-paced basketball. Their enthusiasm under coach Dick Harter and the support they received from their home fans paid off in 20 victories, five games better than the Heat.

But Charlotte fans had to learn to be patient, and that patience was tested in 1989-90 when the club started with five straight losses and finished with a 19-

63 mark. Still, sellout crowds of 23,900 continued to pack Charlotte Coliseum night after night.

The real excitement in Charlotte started in 1991-92 when rookie Larry Johnson of Nevada-Las Vegas came aboard. Johnson, an accurate shooter and powerful rebounder, stepped into the starting lineup immediately, averaging 19 points and 11 rebounds, and provided the inside game the Hornets needed. They stayed in playoff contention until March, but 11 losses in their last 14 games kept them out of postseason play.

But by not making the playoffs, the Hornets wound up with a lottery pick, which they used on Georgetown center Alonzo Mourning. The 6'10" rookie averaged 21 points, 10.3 rebounds, and 3.5 blocks as he helped the Hornets improve to a 44-38 record and claim their first-ever playoff berth in 1992-93. They stung the Boston Celtics in the first round before losing to the Knicks in the Eastern Conference semifinals.

Injuries to Johnson and Mourning stalled the Hornets' rise in 1993-94, but the two stars returned the following season, combining to average 40 points and 16 rebounds. The Hornets won a franchise-record 50 games and returned to the playoffs, only to be eliminated by Michael Jordan and the Chicago Bulls in the first round. The Hornets acquired Kendall Gill in the summer of 1995, but they traded Mourning to the Miami Heat on the eve of the 1995–96 season. In exchange the Hornets got a great shooter in Glen Rice, plus center Matt Geiger and point guard Khalid Reeves.

CHICAGO

CHICAGO BULLS

The 1994-95 season did not end with a fourth championship banner for the Chicago Bulls. But it did mark the return of the incomparable Michael Jordan after his fruitless fling with baseball.

Rejoining the team in March 1995, Jordan played in 17 regular-season games and averaged nearly 27 points. His highlight came at Madison Square Garden when he torched the New York Knicks for 55 points and the game-winning assist at the buzzer. Jordan's heroics ensured a playoff spot for the Bulls, and the team went on to defeat the Charlotte Hornets in the first round of postseason play. But Jordan's rustiness showed in the Eastern Conference semifinals, and the Bulls were ousted by the Orlando Magic in six games.

Such playoff disappointment was a new feeling for the Bulls, who, with Jordan leading the way, won three straight championships in the early 1990s. The most dramatic of the three titles came on June 20, 1993, in Phoenix. The Bulls had a 3-games-to-2 lead in the series but were trailing the Suns, 98-94, with a minute left in Game 6. Jordan's driving layup brought the

Bulls closer and then, after a 24-second violation, John Paxson drilled a 3-point shot with 3.9 seconds left, giving the Bulls their three-peat.

Chicago joined the league in 1966 and surprisingly made the playoffs that season, winning 33 games under coach Johnny "Red" Kerr.

The appointment of Dick Motta as coach in 1968 brought a change in styles for the Bulls. Motta stressed tough team defense and soon they were among the league's best at holding teams under 100 points. That strategy worked as the Bulls, with Bob Love and Chet Walker, won 50 games or more four seasons in a row from 1971 through 1974. Included in that stretch was the Bulls' first-ever playoff series victory, a 7-game elimination of Detroit in 1974.

The Bulls did not win another playoff series until 1981 and did not advance to the conference finals until 1989. By that time, they had made the most important move in team history—the selection of Jordan with the third pick in the 1984 Draft. The former North Carolina star took the league by storm, averaging 28.2 points in his rookie season and thrilling fans all over the league with his incredible moves and dunks.

Jordan went on to lead the league in scoring seven straight times and, of course, take the team to those three consecutive championships under coach Phil Jackson.

The Bulls' quest for a fourth title in 1995-96 got a boost when they obtained rebounder supreme Dennis Rodman from San Antonio just before training camp opened.

CLEVELAND

CAVS™

Unfortunately for the Cavaliers, what could have been the greatest moment in their history turned into the most disappointing.

It was May 7, 1989, and the Cavaliers were playing the Chicago Bulls in the final game of an Eastern Conference playoff series. The Cavaliers, led by Brad Daugherty and Mark Price, had kept their season alive with a 108-105 overtime win at Chicago Stadium two days earlier. Now they were playing for the right to advance in the playoffs.

As the seconds wound down, the Cavaliers held a 100-99 lead, but the Bulls had the ball. They set up a play for Michael Jordan, who was covered closely by Craig Ehlo. With the buzzer about to sound, Jordan cut toward the foul line and went up for a shot. Ehlo followed with him, but Jordan stayed up a split-second longer and arched the ball just over Ehlo's reach. The ball swished through the basket, giving the Bulls the triumph that ended the Cavaliers' season.

Cleveland entered the NBA in 1970-71 and struggled to a 15-67 record, the worst in the league.

Under coach Bill Fitch, the team had 23 wins the next season, 32 the year after that.

The move to a new arena in Richfield, Ohio, and the additions of center Jim Chones and forward Campy Russell helped the Cavaliers in 1975-76. They played stifling defense, limiting opponents to an average of under 100 points per game, and crowds poured into the Coliseum to watch a team that finished with a 49-33 record. In their first playoff series in club history, Cleveland eliminated the Washington Bullets in seven games. Then they took the eventual champion Boston Celtics to six games before losing.

The Cavaliers would not win another playoff series until 1991-92, when after a 57-25 regular season, they defeated the New Jersey Nets and Boston Celtics in back-to-back series before Jordan and his Bulls eliminated them again in the Eastern Conference Finals.

In 1992-93, the Cavaliers reached the Eastern Conference semifinals, only to be ousted once more by the Bulls. They didn't make the playoffs in 1993-94, but they had a change of address in 1994-95—the new Gund Arena in Cleveland.

The new arena didn't help the Cavaliers solve an old problem: injuries. With Brad Daugherty sidelined for the season and Mark Price battling a variety of ailments, Mike Fratello's Cavaliers managed to finish 43-39 and earn a playoff berth.

Entering 1995-96, they were without Price, who was traded to Washington, but gained three-time All-Star Dan Majerle and young Antonio Lang from Phoenix.

DALLAS
MAVERICKS
™

Dallas may be part of the Lone Star State, but there was no doubt that entering the 1995-96 season few NBA teams had as many budding stars as the Dallas Mavericks. In three consecutive years in the early 1990s, the Mavs added Jim Jackson, Jamal Mashburn, and Jason Kidd. In the 1994-95 season Jackson and Mashburn combined to average nearly 50 points per game, and Kidd averaged 11.7 points and 7.7 assists, marks good enough to make him co-Rookie of the Year.

The trio's inspired play helped the Mavericks post an amazing 23-game improvement. After a 13-win season in 1993-94, the Mavs jumped all the way to 36-46 and challenged for a playoff spot until the final month. With the addition of Duke center Cherokee Parks, the Mavs have their sights set on a playoff berth in 1996.

The Mavericks entered the league as an expansion franchise in 1980-81, winning their first game, 103-92, over the eventual Midwest Division champion San Antonio Spurs. But they won only 14 more games the rest of the season. One of them, a 105-95 come-from-behind victory over Utah, prompted coach Dick Motta to say, "This is the best group of pros I ever worked with. I don't think in 20 years I'll be able to say I've ever had a better bunch."

That bunch got better the following season. The Mavericks used their first two picks in the draft to take DePaul's Mark Aguirre and Kansas State's Rolando Blackman, two players who would make their marks. Though Aguirre missed two months of the season with an injury, the Mavericks finished with a 28-54 record, a 13-game improvement over their first year.

The 1982-83 season was a downer, but with the presence of rookies Dale Ellis and Derek Harper, the Mavericks took second in the Midwest Division in 1983-84.

Sam Perkins came aboard in 1984 and Roy Tarpley in 1986, and it was in 1986-87 that Dallas won the Midwest Division with its best record ever, 55-27. But the Mavericks were ousted in the first round of the playoffs by Seattle.

Under new coach John MacLeod in 1987-88, Dallas was 53-29 and on a roll with a team led by Blackman and Aguirre. The Mavericks eliminated Houston and Denver in the playoffs, but fell to the Los Angeles Lakers in a 7-game Western Conference Finals.

Except for 1989-90, when Dallas won 47 games and a playoff berth, it has been largely downhill since then. But the return of coach Dick Motta in 1993-94 and the arrival of the young hopefuls bode well for the future.

From red, white, and blue to tall, taller, and tallest. That's the story of the Denver Nuggets' journey from the old American Basketball Association to being one of the NBA's most exciting young teams in the 1990s.

The addition of 6'9" Alabama forward Antonio McDyess in the summer of 1995 gave the Nuggets one of the biggest lineups in the league. McDyess was expected to team up with 6'8" LaPhonso Ellis, 7'2" Dikembe Mutombo, 6'8" Jalen Rose, and 6'7" Reggie Williams to give Denver a towering, quick starting five that would bring the Nuggets back to the glory days of the spring of 1994. That was when the team became the talk of the NBA with its playoff success.

Those Nuggets, under coach and former NBA player Dan Issel, were a tough, fearless team that very nearly made it to the Western Conference Finals. Issel toned down the fast-breaking style the club was known for in the late 1980s and, instead, put in an offense that made the most of the abilities of 7-foot center Mutombo and guard Mahmoud Abdul-Rauf.

Mutombo averaged only 12 points a game, but finished second in the league in field-goal percentage, was sixth in rebounds, and led the NBA in blocks. He was also the key man in a defense that allowed only 98.8 points per game.

Issel's 1993-94 Nuggets qualified for the playoffs with a 42-40 record, but no one gave them much of a chance against Seattle, seeded No. 1 in the conference after posting a 63-19 mark. After losing the first two games in Seattle, Mutombo, Abdul-Rauf, Ellis and Co. came back to win the series in Game 5.

The Western Conference semifinals against Utah looked like a mismatch as the Nuggets dropped the first three games. But they rallied for three straight victories before yielding to the Jazz.

The 1994-95 Nuggets took a step backward, struggling badly early in the season. Finally, Bernie Bickerstaff, already the team president and general manager, took over as coach in February and led the Nuggets to 20 wins in their final 32 games. That got Denver into the playoffs, where it was beaten by San Antonio in the first round.

The team's history began in the ABA in 1967-68, when they were nicknamed the Rockets. The early days were highlighted by such stars as Ralph Simpson, Mack Calvin, and Larry Jones. Larry Brown became coach in 1974-75, when the Rockets became Nuggets, and he led them to a 65-19 mark and the Western Conference Finals. The addition of David Thompson and Issel in 1975-76 enabled Denver to reach the ABA Finals, where it lost to Julius Erving and his New York Nets.

That was the last season of the ABA, with Denver, the Nets, Indiana, and San Antonio joining the NBA the following year. From then until 1993-94, Denver evolved into a team known for its run-and-gun style that produced not only record numbers of points but also record numbers of points allowed.

Little did Fred Zollner know what effect he would have on professional basketball. Back in 1948, Zollner, president of the Zollner Piston Company, founded an NBA franchise in Fort Wayne, Indiana, and decided to nickname the team the Pistons. More than forty years later, those Pistons, now in Detroit, are mainly responsible for the way the game is played today.

Before the Detroit Pistons started winning consistently in the late 1980s, most NBA teams stressed offense, averaging between 105 and 110 points per game. Coach Chuck Daly knew his Pistons did not have the firepower to match baskets with the league's high-powered offenses, so he had his teams play an aggressive, swarming defense that many teams copied in later years.

The Pistons were known as the "Bad Boys" because of their aggressiveness on defense and their physical play at both ends of the court. Daly rotated three guards—Isiah Thomas, Joe Dumars, and Vinnie Johnson—with a strong frontcourt that featured center Bill Laimbeer and forwards Rick Mahorn, Dennis Rodman, and John Salley.

Were they successful? You bet. The 1987-88 Pistons

came within a whisker of winning the championship. They held a 3-game-to-2 lead on the Los Angeles Lakers in the Finals, but lost Games 6 and 7 in Los Angeles by a combined four points.

The Pistons came into the 1988-89 season determined not to let it happen again. The result was one of the greatest seasons any NBA team ever enjoyed. The Pistons coasted to a 63-19 regular-season record and then rolled through the playoffs.

They swept Boston in three games and Milwaukee in four before running into a challenge from Chicago. They lost two of the first three games to the Michael Jordan-led Bulls before winning three straight. The Lakers again waited for them in the Finals, but this time it was no contest. The Pistons won four straight games to nail down their first championship. They didn't have to wait long for their second, as Daly again led them to the 1990 title with a 5-game triumph over Portland in the Finals.

The success erased the stigma of mediocrity that had followed the club from Fort Wayne through its days at Cobo Hall in downtown Detroit. Though there were some great individual talents (George Yardley, Dave Bing, Bob Lanier), the Pistons never enjoyed much success until Daly took over in 1983-84.

The Pistons faded in the standings after their consecutive titles but had reason to think better times were ahead when rookie Grant Hill came into the league in 1994 and averaged 19.9 points. Hill wound up sharing Rookie-of-the-Year honors with the Mavericks' Jason Kidd. With the emergence of Hill, and the addition of power forward Otis Thorpe in an off-season trade, the Pistons entered the 1995-96 season with renewed hope.

From their start in Philadelphia as an original Basketball Association of America franchise in 1946-47, the Warriors have been a team with a rich tradition. That tradition started when their first team, the Philadelphia Warriors, led by league scoring champion Joe Fulks, won the BAA championship by defeating the Chicago Stags. They won another championship in 1956, then made the move that made the team a contender for years: the signing of center Wilt Chamberlain in 1959.

Chamberlain became the sport's biggest star in his first year with the Warriors. That season he shattered all scoring records by averaging 37.6 points and helping the Warriors improve from 32 to 49 wins. Two years later, Chamberlain averaged a staggering 50.4 points.

Unfortunately for the Warriors, Chamberlain's individual brilliance did not lead to championships because Bill Russell and the Boston Celtics stood in the way. The Celtics ended the Warriors' season three times in a 5-year span, and not even a move to San Francisco in 1962 could change the Warriors' luck.

The Warriors traded Chamberlain to the Philadelphia 76ers in the middle of the 1964-65 season in a shocking deal. The move backfired two years later when Chamberlain led the 76ers to the championship in six games over the Warriors, whose star player was a young forward named Rick Barry.

There were bright moments coming, though. Former Warrior star Al Attles took over as coach late in 1969-70. Barry, who had left the Warriors to join the ABA in 1967, rejoined the team in 1972 and his scoring, playmaking, and defense helped them achieve their greatest triumph in 1975. Barry averaged 30.6 points and 6.2 assists as the Warriors posted a 48-34 record and then defeated Seattle and Chicago to advance to the Finals against the Washington Bullets.

Most experts figured the Bullets would handle the young Warriors, but it didn't happen. With Barry scoring almost at will and feeding Keith Wilkes and Butch Beard, the Warriors stunned the Bullets in four straight games for their only championship since leaving for the West Coast.

The Warriors had a long drought after that, failing to make the playoffs for ten consecutive seasons from 1977 through 1986. They rebounded in 1991-92 as coach Don Nelson guided veteran Chris Mullin and youngsters Tim Hardaway and Billy Owens to a 55-27 record, good for second place in the Pacific Division. But the Warriors' lack of a true center hurt them in the playoffs and in the next couple of seasons. They finally went out and got a big man in Rony Seikaly early in 1994-95 and were hoping that he and No. 1 1995 Draft pick Joe Smith of Maryland would pave the way to NBA gold in the near future.

The Houston Rockets' playoff run in 1995 started slowly, as the team was forced to rally in the closing minutes to overtake Utah in a decisive Game 5 in the first round.

They fell behind Phoenix, three games to one, in the Western Conference semifinals, but Hakeem Olajuwon and Clyde Drexler simply wouldn't let the team lose as the Rockets advanced to the Western Finals against the San Antonio Spurs.

Olajuwon took over, dominating the league's regular-season MVP, David Robinson, in six games as the Rockets made it into the NBA Finals against Orlando.

Most of the experts predicted Houston wouldn't achieve two championships in a row. They were dead wrong. After battling back from a 20-point deficit to win Game 1 in overtime, the Rockets disposed of Shaq O'Neal's Magic in four straight games.

At the finish, beaming with satisfaction, were the old college teammates Olajuwon and Drexler.

The Rockets' long journey to the top of the NBA

began in San Diego in 1967. The expansion Rockets won only 15 of 82 games their first season, but that earned them the right to choose first in the 1968 Draft. They used that pick to take Elvin Hayes, a 6'9" sharpshooter who had starred at the University of Houston. All Hayes did was average 28.4 points and 17.1 rebounds, helping the Rockets improve by 22 games. But the Rockets never really caught on in San Diego and the team moved to Houston in 1971.

Center Moses Malone took the Rockets to the Finals in 1981 and Olajuwon did the same five years later, but both times Houston was beaten by the Larry Bird-led Celtics in six games.

In 1994, with Olajuwon leading the way as regular season and Finals MVP, no one could stop the Rockets. Ditto 1995.

INDIANA

Pacers®

The three biggest things in the state of Indiana every winter are high school basketball, Indiana University basketball, and the Indiana Pacers. In that order. But the Pacers of the mid-1990s demonstrated that the order may be changing. After years of either not making the playoffs or making them but then going out quietly, the Pacers showed signs they may be on the verge of a championship.

The 1993-94 Pacers were the team that started the turnaround. Coach Larry Brown assembled a young, aggressive group that became the NBA's hottest team down the stretch. Reggie Miller, one of the league's most dangerous 3-point shooters, and center Rik Smits gave the Pacers a potent 1-2 scoring punch as the Pacers finished 47-35. The Pacers then demolished the Orlando Magic and Atlanta Hawks in the playoffs before falling to the New York Knicks in a bitterly contested 7-game Eastern Conference Finals.

Undaunted, the Pacers came back stronger than ever in 1994-95. Miller and Smits combined to average 37 points, and Derrick McKey, Dale Davis, and Antonio

Davis provided strong defense and rebounding as the Pacers captured the Central Division crown with a 52-30 record. After eliminating Atlanta in the first round of the playoffs, the Pacers got their revenge against the Knicks by winning a dramatic 7-game series, with the decisive victory coming at Madison Square Garden. Indiana then took the powerful Magic to a 7-game series in the Eastern Conference Finals before falling.

The Pacers' effort won them the kind of support they used to have in the old American Basketball Association days. Those teams—led by Roger Brown, Mel Daniels, and Freddie Lewis—dominated the ABA, winning three championships in a period of four years beginning with 1970.

The transition to the NBA in 1976 was a rough one, as the Pacers did not win a playoff series until the memorable run of 1994.

But with Miller, Smits, McKey, and the Davises all still in their prime, the Pacers' future looked exceptionally bright entering the 1995-96 season.

LOS ANGELES
CLIPPERS ®

You can't blame the Los Angeles Clippers if they suffer from an inferiority complex. Most NBA clubs would have the same complex if they had to share their home city with the Los Angeles Lakers. Being good isn't good enough when your intracity rivals are perennial NBA title contenders. Still, the Clippers have had a few bright moments.

After years of playing second fiddle while the Lakers were becoming the NBA's dominant team of the 1980s, the Clippers made the rest of the league notice them in 1991-92. With Ron Harper and Mark Jackson forming an explosive backcourt, and Danny Manning and Ken Norman providing the in-close points and rebounds, the Clippers became a legitimate playoff contender. A midseason coaching switch to Larry Brown helped, too, as the Clippers finished at 45-37, ahead of their arch-rival Lakers for the first time. This gave the Clippers their first playoff berth since 1975-76, when the team was based in Buffalo.

In 1992-93, Manning became one of the league's brightest stars, averaging 22.8 points, and Harper chipped in with 18.0 points and 4.5 assists as the Clippers finished 41-41. In the playoffs they gave No. 2 seed Houston all it could handle before dropping an 84-80 decision in the fifth game at the Summit.

The 1993-94 season was one of change for the Clippers. Manning, who would have been a free agent at the end of the season, was traded to Atlanta for Dominique Wilkins. Wilkins averaged 29.1 points in his 25 games with the Clippers but was unable to salvage what would wind up as a 27-55 season.

Wilkins left for Boston at the end of that season, leaving the Clippers with a hole that was impossible to fill. Though forwards Loy Vaught (17.5 ppg) and rookie Lamond Murray (14.1) were strong night after night, the Clippers finished with an NBA-worst 17-65 record. The off-season additions of Rodney Rogers and rookie Brent Barry gave the team renewed hope entering 1995-96.

Some of the Clippers' brightest days came in the very beginning, when they were based in Buffalo and were known as the Braves. They entered the league in 1970 and, within five years, became a contender. The turning point came in the 1972 Draft when the Braves added Bob McAdoo, a 6'9" jump-shooting machine who quickly became a fixture among the league leaders in scoring.

With McAdoo averaging 30.6 points per game, the 1973-74 Braves finished 42-40, then took the powerful Boston Celtics to six games before losing in the playoffs. The next season the Braves won a club-record 49 games, and in the playoffs took the Washington Bullets to seven games before falling.

The 1975-76 Braves hold the honor as the only

team in franchise history to win a playoff series. McAdoo averaged 31.1 points as the team finished 46-36, then ousted the 76ers in the first round. But a loss to the Celtics followed, and three years later the Braves were on their way to San Diego. They moved to Los Angeles in 1984.

Los Angeles is not known for its lakes, but the state of Minnesota is, and that's how a team based in L.A. ended up with a nickname borrowed from another state at another time. The original Lakers played in Minneapolis and entered the NBA in 1949. It didn't take long for the club to build a tradition of excellence as George Mikan, the first of the NBA's great big men, led the team to the league championship in its first season. Mikan's dominance made the Lakers the league's first dynasty, with five championships in a 6-year stretch.

The Lakers gave the NBA its first presence on the West Coast when they moved to Los Angeles for the 1960-61 season. If not for the Boston Celtics, the Lakers of the 1960s might have duplicated the success of the early Minneapolis teams. But the Celtics defeated the Lakers in the Finals six times in an 8-year span. Those Laker teams, which featured Elgin Baylor and Jerry West, became known as some of the greatest never to win a title. Not even a trade for Wilt Chamberlain in 1968 could change the Lakers' fortune in the Finals.

The first West Coast title finally came in 1972. Chamberlain combined with West, Gail Goodrich, Jim McMillian, and Happy Hairston on a team that set an NBA record with 33 straight wins in the regular season and then coasted through the playoffs, winning 12 of 15 games.

The retirement of West, Baylor, and Chamberlain led to some down years, but the Lakers recovered by trading with Milwaukee for Kareem Abdul-Jabbar in 1975. The 7'2" center, who would become the game's all-time leading scorer, kept the Lakers respectable until the drafting of Earvin "Magic" Johnson in 1979. The 6'9" Johnson immediately became the league's tallest and most dangerous point guard. He even filled in at center in Game 6 of the 1980 Finals against the 76ers, and his 42 points led the Lakers to their first championship in eight years.

The Lakers' fast-breaking style became known as Showtime, and Los Angeles became known as the Titletown of the NBA. With Abdul-Jabbar and Johnson joined by James Worthy and Byron Scott, the Lakers went on to win four more championships in the 1980s.

Abdul-Jabbar retired in 1989 and Johnson did the same two years later, forcing Lakers executive vice president Jerry West to rebuild. He did so in 1994-95 with flashy guard Nick Van Exel, sure-shooting forward Cedric Ceballos, center Vlade Divac, and rookie Eddie Jones. The four led the Lakers to a surprising 48-34 record. Then the young Lakers went out and stunned the Seattle Sonics in the first round of the playoffs before seeing their season ended by the San Antonio Spurs. Still, the rest of the NBA knew that Showtime was back.

MIAMI HEAT

On September 3, 1995, a new era began for the Miami Heat when they named Pat Riley as president, coach, and part-owner of the franchise.

Riley needs little introduction. As the winningest coach in NBA playoff history, his trophy chest includes four championship rings as head coach of the Lakers, another as an assistant with the Lakers, and a sixth title ring with the Lakers as a player.

He joined the Heat after four years with the Knicks, and he brings hope and enthusiasm to a team that has had little to cheer about since it began life in the 1988-89 season. That was the year rookies Rony Seikaly and Kevin Edwards gained valuable experience, but the Heat won only 15 games.

Glen Rice and Sherman Douglas were added in the 1989 Draft and Miami managed to win 18 games as the fans continued to support the team. There were sellouts at every game in Miami Arena.

Willie Burton (1990) and Steve Smith (1991) joined the Heat in the next two Drafts, and now all the pieces were in place for a run at a playoff spot. With Rice's long-range shooting and Seikaly's inside game providing a 1-2 punch, the 1991-92 Heat won 28 of 41 home games to finish at 38-44 and make the playoffs. They then lost three straight games to the eventual champion Chicago Bulls.

After not making the playoffs in 1992-93, the Heat had their best season in 1993-94, finishing over .500 (42-40) for the first time. The core of the team was Rice, Smith, and Seikaly, and they weren't satisfied with simply making the playoffs. They threw a giant scare into the East's top seed, Atlanta, in the first round, before losing in five games.

Miami made major changes in 1994-95. Smith was traded to Atlanta and Seikaly went to Golden State, with Kevin Willis and Billy Owens joining them in the lineup. But the Heat finished 32-50, three games out of the final Eastern Conference playoff slot. The highlight of the season was Rice burning the Magic for 56 points in a nationally-televised game.

Not making the playoffs helped the Heat better their draft position in 1995 and they came up with a gem in Texas Christian's Kurt Thomas, a 6'9" forward.

But the big news in 1995-96, apart from the coming of a super-coach named Riley, was the preseason trade that brought Alonzo Mourning from the Charlotte Hornets. The Heat had to give up Rice, Matt Geiger, Khalid Reeves, and a 1996 first-round draft pick in the process.

MILWAUKEE
BUCKS

You look at the Milwaukee Bucks' records in the 1990s and you see mediocrity. A 20-win season. A 28-win season. And a 34-win campaign. And then you look at the young talent coach Mike Dunleavy has assembled, and suddenly you can see a team that is working its way back up to NBA respectability. With Glenn Robinson, Vin Baker, Todd Day, Eric Murdock, and rookie Shawn Respert, the word around the NBA in the beginning of the 1995-96 season was that the Bucks were back.

The team entered the NBA as an expansion franchise in 1968-69 and suffered through growing pains. A 27-55 record left them in last place in the Eastern Division but put them in position to draft Kareem Abdul-Jabbar of UCLA, the most dominant college player of his generation. To get the rights to Abdul-Jabbar, all the Bucks would have to do was win a coin flip with the Phoenix Suns, who also entered the league that season and had finished in last place in the Western Division.

The Suns called heads, the coin came up tails, and Abdul-Jabbar was on his way to Milwaukee. The 7'2" center's impact on the league was incredible. The

Bucks went from 27 to 56 wins and challenged the New York Knicks for the Eastern Division title while Abdul-Jabbar finished second in the league in scoring (28.8) and third in rebounds (13.5).

As it turned out, the young Bucks didn't have enough to win a championship. They defeated the Philadelphia 76ers in the first round of the 1970 playoffs but were beaten by the Knicks in the Eastern Conference Finals. The defeat convinced the Bucks they needed one more superstar to reach the top. During the offseason, that superstar came when the Bucks acquired Oscar Robertson from the Cincinnati Royals.

The Robertson/Abdul-Jabbar combination quickly proved to be too much for the rest of the NBA. In 1970-71, the Bucks finished with a league-best 66-16 record and won the Midwest Division by a whopping 15 games. In the playoffs, the Bucks romped past San Francisco and Los Angeles before blowing out the Baltimore Bullets in four straight in the Finals. That gave the Bucks the championship in only their third season, faster than any team in any professional sport.

The next season, the Bucks didn't get beyond the Western Conference Finals, losing to the Lakers. Two years later, in 1974, they almost won a second title, but Boston defeated the Bucks in Game 7.

Even after the departure of Abdul-Jabbar to Los Angeles in a 1975 trade, the Bucks went on to dominate the Central Division. With Sidney Moncrief and Terry Cummings, they won six straight division crowns from 1980-81 through 1985-86. They went to the Conference Finals three times, only to lose each time.

Milwaukee fans now believe that a new era is about to begin.

Never has an NBA team ever attracted more fan support than the Minnesota Timberwolves did in 1989-90, their first season. Playing in the spacious Metrodome while waiting for their own arena to be built, the Timberwolves attracted 1,072,572 fans to their home games, a per-game average of 26,160.

The fans showed their support of a defense-oriented club that won only 22 times, but held its opponents to an average of only 99.4 points. Offensively, the star was Tony Campbell, a veteran forward who had arrived in the expansion draft and averaged 23.2 points.

Campbell was nearly as strong the following season and his teammates were more effective. They won six of their final eight games to finish at 29-53.

But in 1991-92 the T-Wolves struggled to a 4-23 mark in the first two months of the season and then a 16-game losing streak later in the campaign ensured that they would have their worst record ever. The bright spot was that Minnesota wound up with the third pick in the lottery and they used that on Duke All-American Christian Laettner, a 6'11" forward who had been the first collegian in history to start in four NCAA Tournament Final Fours.

The addition of Laettner, the improvement of Doug West, and a preseason trade with Indiana that brought in Chuck Person and Micheal Williams made the T-Wolves much more competitive in 1992-93. Laettner was named to the All-Rookie Team after averaging 18.2 points and 8.7 assists, and West, in his fourth season, averaged a career-high 19.3 points as the T-Wolves finished at 19-63. One highlight was Williams breaking Calvin Murphy's NBA record by making 84 consecutive free throws in the final month.

The 1993 Draft brought in Isaiah (J.R.) Rider from Nevada-Las Vegas, and he combined with Lacttner to give Minnesota one of the best young frontcourts in the league. Rider, who won the Slam-Dunk contest at All-Star Weekend, averaged 16.6 points, second on the club behind Laettner's 16.8, and the T-Wolves improved to 20-62. Williams, meanwhile, extended his streak of consecutive free throws to 97 before missing early in the 1993-94 season.

The T-Wolves got new ownership before the 1994-95 season, avoiding a possible move to New Orleans. On the court the team struggled with a 21-61 record despite the addition of forward Tom Gugliotta in a midseason trade. With the drafting of high school sensation Kevin Garnett, the T-Wolves felt they had the makings of a solid, young starting five.

The New Jersey Nets have been a saga of triumph and tragedy since they came into the NBA as one of the four American Basketball Association franchises in 1976. Much of the triumph came in the mid-1970s, when the team was still in the ABA and based on Long Island as the New York Nets. The Nets had put together a team built around forward Julius Erving, a local product who was the most spectacular player of his generation.

Dr. J was known for his incredible leaping ability and soaring dunks. The Nets took full advantage of his ability, using a fast-break style that often ended in a windmill slam dunk by Erving. With Larry Kenon at the other forward, Billy Paultz at center, and John Williamson at guard, the Nets built a team that won two of the last three ABA championships.

But a contract dispute prompted owner Roy Boe to send Erving to the 76ers before the Nets' first NBA season started in 1976, and the team's hopes of competing in the expanded league vanished. After a 22-60 record, Boe moved the team to New Jersey, where the fans had the pleasure of seeing rookie Bernard King average 24.2 points and 9.5 rebounds.

The early 1980s were the Nets' finest years in the NBA. With young forward Buck Williams and Albert King playing alongside dynamic center Darryl Dawkins, the Nets made the playoffs five straight times.

The 1983-84 team was the only one to win a playoff series, though, and it was memorable. The Nets had won 19 of their last 25 games, then stunned the defending champion Philadelphia 76ers in the first round of the playoffs. Their season was ended by the Milwaukee Bucks in the next round.

But a series of injuries ruined the Nets in the late 1980s. Dawkins, Otis Birdsong, Keith Lee, and Joe Barry Carroll were all sidelined by major ailments and the Nets' hopes skidded.

Just when it seemed the Nets were turning things around, tragedy struck. The team had rebuilt behind forward Derrick Coleman and guard Kenny Anderson and made the playoffs in both 1992 and 1993. But after the 1992-93 season, starting guard Drazen Petrovic was killed in an automobile accident, leaving the Nets with a huge hole to fill.

Despite the tragic loss, the 1993-94 Nets managed to make the playoffs and throw a scare into the Knicks in a tough, 4-game series in the first round.

But the injury jinx struck repeatedly the following season as Coleman, Kevin Edwards, and rookie Yinka Dare all missed large parts of what became a 30-52 season. The Nets were hoping that rookie Ed O'Bannon and the return to health by several of their key players would spark a resurgence in 1995-96.

NEW YORK KNICKS

The New York Knicks, who entered the league as one of its charter members in 1946, have had many proud moments in their long tenure, but none was prouder than the night of May 7, 1970. It was on that night that Willis Reed led them to their first NBA championship.

It was Game 7 of the Finals between the Knicks and the Los Angeles Lakers, and the Knicks knew their hopes of winning the title depended on the condition of their 6'10" center and captain. Reed had injured his hip in a collision in Game 5, and no one knew if he would be ready to return for the decisive seventh game. The Knicks had battled back without Reed to win Game 5 but were routed in Game 6 in Los Angeles, tying the series.

The teams came out to warm up for Game 7, but there was no Reed. Not even the other Knicks knew if he'd be playing. Suddenly, about five minutes before tipoff, a roar went up from the crowd. They had spotted Reed coming through the tunnel onto the court. The inspired Knicks knew there was no stopping them now.

Their center hit his first two shots to stake them to an early lead, and then Walt Frazier chipped in with 36 points and 19 assists to propel the Knicks to a 113-99 victory and their first NBA championship.

That title erased years of frustration for the Knicks, who had made it to the Finals three straight times in the early 1950s, only to lose each time. After winning in 1970, the Knicks challenged for another title the next three years, losing in the Finals in 1972, then winning over the Lakers in 1973.

After some down years, the Knicks started rebuilding in 1985, with a little luck. In the NBA's first lottery, they won the right to draft Georgetown center Patrick Ewing, who would go on to become one of the league's most dominant big men.

Ewing played only 50 games his rookie season due to injuries but still averaged 20 points and 9 rebounds. Ewing's presence helped the Knicks make the playoffs in his third season, and then trades for Charles Oakley and Charles Smith, and the improvement of former CBA players John Starks and Anthony Mason made the Knicks serious contenders in the 1990s.

With former Lakers coach Pat Riley at the helm, the Knicks had several chances to return to their glory days. But they lost to the eventual champion Chicago Bulls in 1992 and 1993, lost a 7-game Finals series to Houston in 1994, and then were beaten by the Indiana Pacers in a 7-game second-round series in 1995.

In the aftermath of the season, Riley resigned from the Knicks and subsequently signed with the Miami Heat. Ex-Bucks and Warriors coach Don Nelson replaced Riley as coach of the Knicks.

If the 1994-95 season was an indication, the rest of the National Basketball Association can plan on watching the Orlando Magic celebrate a title in the near future.

The Magic, one of the youngest teams in the league, came within four wins of their first championship in 1995. With Shaquille O'Neal winning the scoring title with an average of 29.3, point guard Penny Hardaway contributing 20.9 points and 7.2 assists, and ex-Bull Horace Grant adding to the mix, the Magic coasted to the Atlantic Division title with a 57-25 record. This included an incredible 39-2 record at home.

For awhile, the playoffs were a joyride, too, as the Magic ousted the Celtics, Bulls, and Pacers in the first three rounds.

But the Finals were another story as the Houston Rockets took advantage of the young Magic's inexperience. Orlando blew a 20-point lead and lost Game 1 in overtime and never recovered, with the Rockets polishing them off in four straight games.

The key to Orlando's success was luck in the NBA's

Draft lottery. The team entered the league in 1989 and within two years posted a respectable 31-win season. But they relapsed in 1991-92, winning only 21 games but also winning the top draft pick. That pick turned out to be the 7'1" O'Neal. The big center's presence helped the Magic improve all the way to 41-41 in his rookie season, but the team's record was not good enough to earn a playoff spot.

The Magic beat the odds, winning the lottery again in 1993. They used the pick on Michigan's Chris Webber, then traded him to the Golden State Warriors for the rights to Hardaway and three future first-round picks. The combination of O'Neal and Hardaway with sharpshooters Nick Anderson and Dennis Scott jelled quickly as the Magic rolled to a 50-32 record and their first playoff berth in 1994. But the season ended with a first-round playoff sweep by Indiana.

During the off-season in 1995, the Magic got additional strength when they drafted power forward David Vaughn from Memphis.

The city of Philadelphia has always been known for the Liberty Bell, cheesesteaks, and pretzels with mustard. And for much of the past 30 years it's been known for good basketball, too.

The 76ers are one of the NBA's charter franchises. They started play as the Syracuse Nationals in the Basketball Association of America in 1946. Those days in Syracuse were memorable for the crowds, who used to involve themselves in the action by shaking the guidewires to the basket while a Nationals' opponent was shooting free throws.

Not that the Nationals needed that much help; the 1954-55 team, led by forward Dolph Schayes (whose son Dan would later play in the NBA), won the league championship with a 7-game triumph over the Fort Wayne Pistons. The club moved to the City of Brotherly Love in 1963, partly to fill the void left by the Philadelphia Warriors, who had moved to San Francisco.

Once in Philadelphia, the Nationals renamed themselves the 76ers and started building one of the toughest teams in the NBA. Two years after the move, the 76ers stunned the NBA by obtaining Wilt Chamberlain from the Warriors in a multi-player deal. The addition of Chamberlain to a team that already had Hal Greer, Lucius Jackson, and Chet Walker made the 76ers championship contenders.

The 1966-67 team, which is regarded as one of the great teams in NBA history, broke through the Celtics' domination and ended their streak of eight straight championships. Chamberlain averaged "only" 24 points but contributed 24 rebounds and 7.8 assists per game as the 76ers won 68 of 81 games, then ousted Cincinnati, Boston, and San Francisco to bring the championship to Philadelphia.

The 76ers had to wait 16 years for another title. The 1982-83 team, led by Julius Erving and Moses Malone, had a league-best 65-17 record in the regular season. Malone said before the playoffs that the 76ers would win in "four, four, and four" and he was nearly right. The team dropped only 1 of 13 games in rolling to the title over New York, Milwaukee, and Los Angeles.

The 76ers have not come close to winning another title since then, despite the presence of Charles Barkley from 1984 through 1992. The 1994-95 team won only 24 games but got impressive performances from guard Dana Barros, who was voted the NBA's Most Improved Player (now with Boston), and 7'6" center Shawn Bradley, who finished third in the league in blocked-shots average. With the addition of first-round draft pick Jerry Stackhouse of North Carolina, the 76ers felt they had a strong core for the 1995-96 season.

Say one thing for the Phoenix Suns: when they make it to the NBA Finals, you know it will be a memorable series.

Take 1992-93, for example. The Suns, led by Charles Barkley and Kevin Johnson, rolled to an NBA-best 62-20 regular-season record and then disposed of the Lakers, Spurs, and Sonics en route to a date with the Michael Jordan-led Chicago Bulls in the Finals.

The series looked like a rout in the early stages as the Bulls, who were seeking their third straight championship, won Games 1 and 2. "We're in a big hole right now, and we're in the right state for big holes," Barkley said after Game 2, referring to Arizona's Grand Canyon.

Dan Majerle (now with Cleveland) helped them climb back into the series with six 3-pointers as the Suns battled back from an 11-point, fourth-quarter deficit, and finally outlasted the Bulls, 129-121, in triple overtime. The Bulls, however, won Game 4 and were all set to wrap up the title because Game 5 was to be played at Chicago Stadium.

But the Suns wouldn't die quietly. Forward Richard Dumas broke loose for 25 points as the Suns staved off elimination with a 108-98 win in Game 5, sending the series back to Phoenix. The Suns were on the verge of forcing a seventh game, too, but John Paxson's 3-point shot with 3.9 seconds left gave the Bulls a 99-98 victory.

The Suns' other trip to the Finals was equally dramatic. The year was 1976 and the Suns' rise was much more of a surprise. They finished the regular season 42-40, 17 games behind Pacific Division winner Golden State, but played their best basketball in the playoffs.

The Suns upset Seattle in the first round and then shocked the basketball world by eliminating the Warriors in seven games in the Western Conference Finals. That brought them up against the powerful Boston Celtics, who were seeking their 13th NBA title.

The teams split the first four games, then staged one of the most exciting Finals games in history. The Suns twice hit clutch baskets to force overtimes before the Celtics finally prevailed, 128-126, in a third overtime. Boston then wrapped up the series in Phoenix.

The 1994-95 Suns felt they had a legitimate chance at a title, but an injury to Danny Manning hampered them down the stretch of the regular season and in the playoffs. The Suns managed to win 59 games, but without Manning, and with Barkley and Kevin Johnson recovering from injuries, they were beaten by Houston in the second round of the playoffs.

PORTLAND BLAZERS ™

The times, they are changing in Portland. In the 1990s the Trail Blazers turned the page on their past with a new coach (P.J. Carlesimo), a new superstar (Clifford Robinson), and a new arena. Carlesimo took over in 1994-95 and guided the Blazers to a 44-38 record, good enough for a playoff berth. The Blazers' season ended with a first-round sweep by Phoenix, but Carlesimo quickly established himself as one of the NBA's brightest young coaches. Rookie Gary Trent was added in the off-season to strengthen the Blazers' frontline for 1995-96.

The Trail Blazers started play in the NBA in 1970, but most veteran fans point to 1974 as the team's jumping-off point.

It was in the 1974 Draft that the Blazers claimed a center from UCLA named Bill Walton, who had led the Bruins to two national championships and three Final Fours in three years. Walton played only parts of five seasons with the Blazers due to a series of injuries, but while he was there he was in the middle of the greatest Trail Blazer team in history.

In 1976-77, Walton teamed with Maurice Lucas, Bobby

Gross, Dave Twardzik, and Lionel Hollins to take the Blazers to a 49-33 record and their first playoff berth. The team didn't have overwhelming talent but, with Walton manning the post, played brilliant team basketball.

Once they got to the playoffs, the Blazers were, well, blazing. They ousted the Chicago Bulls in three straight games, then upset Midwest Division champion Denver in six. Few gave them a chance against Kareem Abdul-Jabbar and the powerful Lakers, but the Walton Gang was now unstoppable and they blew past L.A. in four straight games.

Waiting for them in the Finals were the powerful Philadelphia 76ers, led by Julius Erving and Darryl Dawkins. Portland dropped the first two games in Philadelphia but then tied the series by scoring 129 and 130 points in two games back home.

In Game 5, the Blazers built a big lead in the third quarter, then held off a 76er rally to win, 110-104. This close to the title, Portland wasn't about to let it slip away. The Blazers had a 12-point lead with 5 minutes left and again had to withstand a 76ers rally. But with the Blazers holding a 109-107 lead with 18 seconds left, Erving and George McGinnis of the Sixers missed shots and the buzzer sounded. The Blazers were champions.

Portland has been back to the Finals twice since then. The 1989-90 team, led by Clyde "The Glide" Drexler and Terry Porter, won 59 regular-season games, then ousted Dallas, San Antonio, and Phoenix to advance to the Finals. But after gaining a split of the first two games in Detroit, the Blazers lost three straight at home and were eliminated. In 1992, Portland won the Pacific Division title and rolled into the Finals, where they were beaten by Michael Jordan and the Bulls in six games.

Rochester. Cincinnati. Kansas City-Omaha. Kansas City. Sacramento. Yes, the Kings have certainly been around in their years in the NBA. And through all their moves there has been one constant: great play from their guards.

Mitch Richmond is the latest in a string of Kings guards who have left their mark on the NBA. Richmond, a 6'5" scorer acquired from Golden State, averaged better than 21 points per game in his first four seasons in Sacramento. In 1994-95, his 22.8 points-per-game average was eighth-best in the league and helped the Kings stay in the running for a playoff berth until the final month of the season.

Richmond follows a franchise tradition started by Bob Davies and carried on by Oscar Robertson, Nate Archibald, and Otis Birdsong. Davies was the club's sparkplug in the early days, when the team was based in Rochester and nicknamed the Royals. In 1950-51, he averaged 15.2 points and led the team in assists as the Royals won the only championship in franchise history. The Royals finished second in the Western

Division with a 41-27 record, then defeated the Fort Wayne Pistons, Minneapolis Lakers, and the New York Knicks to capture the championship.

The team moved to Cincinnati in 1957 and Robertson came along three years later, after a sensational career at the University of Cincinnati. "The Big O" was a unanimous selection as Rookie of the Year after averaging 30.6 points, 10.1 rebounds, and 9.7 assists, and helping the Royals improve from 19 to 33 wins.

The following season he became the only player in history to average double figures in points, rebounds, and assists. Robertson and Jerry Lucas combined on some fine teams that might have won championships in the mid-1960s if not for the dominance of the Boston Celtics.

Robertson was traded to Milwaukee in 1970, just in time for Nate "Tiny" Archibald to take over. In 1971-72, the team's first season as the Kansas City-Omaha Kings, Archibald became the first player in history to lead the NBA in scoring and assists. The small, quick Archibald averaged 25.2 points and 8.1 assists in six seasons with the club.

Birdsong joined the team in 1977-78. He spent only four seasons with the Kings but led the club in scoring the last three.

Since moving from Kansas City to Sacramento in 1985, the Kings have never finished higher than fifth in their division. But the 39-win season of 1994-95 and the additions of rookies Corliss Williamson and Tyus Edney in 1995 gave the Kings reasons for some optimism.

The history of the San Antonio Spurs can be divided into two chapters: before David Robinson and after David Robinson. How important is Robinson to the Spurs? Well, consider these arguments: The 1988-89 Spurs had a 21-61 record and were a dreadful 3-38 on the road. The following season, with the rookie Robinson manning the center position, the Spurs finished 56-26. Their 35-game improvement is the largest in NBA history.

Robinson was a unanimous choice as Rookie of the Year in 1990, after averaging 24.3 points, 12 rebounds, and 3.9 blocks. He combined with forwards Terry Cummings and Willie Anderson on a frontline that averaged 61 points per game. The Spurs finished the season with a rush, winning 19 of their last 27 games, then defeated the Denver Nuggets in three straight in the first round of the playoffs. The young Spurs took eventual Western Conference champion Portland into overtime of a seventh game before succumbing.

Robinson and the Spurs have gotten better and better in the 1990s. The big center won the scoring title in 1993-94, averaging 29.8 points, including 71 in the final game of the season to edge out Shaquille O'Neal for the No. 1 spot. The following season Robinson's 27.6 average was third in the league, he was named the NBA's MVP, and the Spurs won a league-best 62 games. Robinson combined with Dennis Rodman, Sean Elliott, and Avery Johnson to help the Spurs defeat the Denver Nuggets and Los Angeles Lakers and advance to the Western Conference Finals, where they were defeated by Houston.

Robinson was the second Spur to win a scoring title with a last-day barrage. George "Ice" Gervin, one of the NBA's best players in the late 1970s and early 1980s, won scoring honors in 1977-78 by scoring 63 points in the final game of the regular season. He needed almost every one of them because the Nuggets' David Thompson, who would finish second, scored 73 earlier that day. It was the first of three straight scoring titles for Gervin.

The Spurs were one of the old American Basketball Association teams, starting play as the Dallas Chapparals in 1967. They moved to San Antonio in 1973, then joined the Nets, Pacers, and Nuggets as NBA teams three years later. In the first season after the merger, the Spurs played much of the season without their best player, guard James Silas, and still made the playoffs with a 44-38 record.

Once Gervin left after the 1984-85 season, the Spurs struggled until Robinson came along.

SEATTLE

TM
© 1994 NBAP

If only regular-season success guaranteed wins in the playoffs, the Seattle Sonics would have been fitted for championship rings in the 1990s. In the 1993-94 and 1994-95 seasons, the Sonics won a combined 120 games in the regular season, only to see their title hopes smashed in the first round by lower-seeded teams.

In 1993-94, Seattle had the best record (63-19) in the league and won its first two playoff games against the Denver Nuggets. But the Nuggets stormed back and won three straight, ending the Sonics' season. In 1994-95, Seattle's 57-25 record tied for fourth-best in the league. Again it wasn't enough as the Sonics were beaten by the Los Angeles Lakers in a four-game, first-round series. With Shawn Kemp and Gary Payton leading the way, the 1995-96 Sonics were hoping the new season would not end as early as those in the recent past.

Once, though, the season did not end too early. It was 1978-79, and the Sonics, under coach Lenny Wilkens, had become an NBA powerhouse. They had made it to the Finals the year before, only to be upset by the Washington Bullets in seven games.

The Sonics had an unusually flexible and cohesive 7-man unit, with John Johnson and Lonnie Shelton at forward, Jack Sikma at center, Dennis Johnson and Gus Williams in the backcourt, and Paul Silas and Fred "Downtown" Brown coming off the bench. They won the Pacific Division title with a 50-32 record and then it was on to the playoffs.

Seattle took out the Lakers in five games and squeezed past the Suns in seven to gain a rematch against the Bullets in the Finals. This time, however, the result was different: The Sonics lost the first game, but swept the next four, and Seattle had its championship.

Seattle entered the league as an expansion team in 1967 and suffered through the same growing pains most teams have in their early years. Forward Spencer Haywood, their leading scorer five straight seasons, kept them competitive until the core of the championship team could be built.

Isiah Thomas, familiar to basketball fans everywhere as a superstar during his 13-year career with the Detroit Pistons, has a new challenge as the vice president of basketball operations with a new NBA team, the Toronto Raptors.

They began play in Toronto's SkyDome as the 28th franchise in the NBA in the 1995-96 season. The ownership group is headed by John Bitove, Jr.

The Raptors took B.J. Armstrong (since traded to Golden State), Tony Massenburg, Andres Guibert, and Dontonio Wingfield as their top picks in the expansion draft, then added Arizona's Damon Stoudamire and Michigan's Jimmy King in the college draft. Coach Brendan Malone was hoping a change of scenery would work wonders for veteran John Salley and former Warriors Victor Alexander and Carlos Rogers, obtained in the trade for Armstrong.

How in the world did a team with the nickname Jazz end up in Utah? By starting in New Orleans, that's how.

Formed in 1974, the Jazz spent their first five seasons down on the bayou. Their first move was one of the best in team history—the acquisition of guard Pete Maravich, who had starred at Louisiana State and was regarded as a folk hero in the area. But as good as Maravich was (a league-leading 31.1 points per game in 1976-77), the Jazz were unable to surround him with enough talent to make the playoffs.

After failing in their playoff quest, the team moved to Utah in 1979 and decided to keep the nickname Jazz, even though it was not particularly suited to the region where the Mormon faith was born. It took until 1983-84 for the Jazz to make the playoffs, but when they did it, they did it in a big way.

That year the Jazz won the Midwest Division title with a 45-37 record and became the first team in history to have four players win individual titles. Forward Adrian Dantley won the scoring championship

(30.6), center Mark Eaton led in blocks (4.28), guard Darrell Griffith was the 3-point percentage leader (.361), and guard Rickey Green was tops in steals (2.65). The Jazz won their first-ever playoff series, defeating the Nuggets in five games before losing to the Suns in a 6-game Western Conference semifinal series.

The Jazz of the 1990s always seemed to be on the verge of greatness but failed to take the step that would put them in the Finals.

The 1991-92 team was one of the best in franchise history, winning the Midwest Division championship with a 55-27 record. With John Stockton running the show (a league-best 13.7 assists per game) and forward Karl Malone providing scoring (28.0) and rebounding (11.2), the Jazz roared into the playoffs.

They defeated the Clippers and then wiped out the Sonics in five games to advance to the Western Conference Finals against Portland. But after climbing back from a 2-game deficit to tie the series, the Jazz lost a pivotal fifth game in overtime in Portland. The Blazers then closed out the series with a victory in Utah in Game 6.

The 1994-95 Jazz nearly changed the course of history. They had the Rockets down by eight points in the final quarter of their Game 5 first-round matchup, only to see the Rockets come back, win the series, and go on to capture their second straight championship. Stockton, now the NBA's all-time assist king, and Malone were back in 1995-96 looking to take that next step.

Hockey may be the national sport of Canada, but basketball made its inroads in the 1995-96 season with the addition of the Toronto Raptors and Vancouver Grizzlies. A group headed by Arthur Griffith was granted the franchise in Vancouver, which housed a fine new arena named General Motors Place.

Former Knicks coach Stu Jackson was named vice president and general manager of the team, and longtime NBA assistant Brian Winters was appointed the franchise's first coach.

Winters went into the first season with a roster that featured veterans Gerald Wilkins, Greg Anthony, Blue Edwards, and Byron Scott, and first-round pick Bryant "Big Country" Reeves.

"The opera isn't over till the fat lady sings." That's the motto that sparked the Washington Bullets to their greatest moment of glory—the 1978 NBA championship.

Ironically, this was a year the Bullets were given little chance to win a title. It was the 1974-75 team that was supposed to win; that team coasted to the Central Division title with a 60-22 record. Elvin Hayes, a 6'9" smooth-shooting forward, was at the peak of his game, averaging 23 points and finishing eighth in rebounds and fourth in blocks.

With Wes Unseld rebounding and setting picks, and league assist leader Kevin Porter running the offense, the Bullets were odds-on favorites to capture their first title. But after defeating Buffalo in seven games and Boston in six, the Bullets ran into a roadblock in the Finals, with the Golden State Warriors stunning them four straight times to take the championship.

The 1977-78 team gave little hint of what was to come. Hayes and Unseld were still there, and the addition of forward Bob Dandridge gave the Bullets another scoring threat. But the Bullets finished the regular season with only 44 wins, tied for eighth in the overall standings, and thoughts of a championship seemed pretty far-fetched.

Even after playoff wins over Atlanta, San Antonio, and Philadelphia, the Bullets' task appeared too tough. They fell behind the Seattle Sonics two games to one and had to play the next two games in Seattle. When asked if it was over, the Bullets responded with their battle cry, "It ain't over till the fat lady sings."

They were right. The Bullets won Game 4 in overtime to earn the split they needed in Seattle. Then, down 3-2, they trounced the Sonics, 117-82, back at home and then won again, 105-99, in Seattle to bring the title back to Washington. It was the last time any team won Game 7 of the Finals on the road.

The birth of the Bullets actually was in Chicago, back in 1961. The expansion Chicago Packers (who later changed their nickname to Zephyrs) spent their early years in the Windy City before moving to Baltimore and becoming the Bullets in 1963. They became known as the Capital Bullets in 1974 before becoming the Washington Bullets the following year.

The Bullets spent much of the 1990s in a rebuilding mode. Though they won only 21 games in 1994-95, the Bullets had a solid core of young players in former Michigan superstars Chris Webber and Juwan Howard, 7'7" center George Muresan and young swingman Calbert Cheaney. Former North Carolina star Rasheed Wallace was added in the college draft, giving coach Jim Lynam another good young player. The Bullets' lineup was further strengthened in 1995-96 with the addition of former Cavalier point guard Mark Price.

The Basketball Hall of Fame

— — —

He started it all in Springfield, Massachusetts, with a peach basket. That was more than 100 years ago, in 1891, when Dr. James Naismith invented the game of basketball.

Not far from the original site in Springfield is the Naismith Memorial Basketball Hall of Fame.

It is a modern, 3-level structure on the banks of the Connecticut River and it has something for basketball fans from 8 to 80.

Honored here are the sport's immortals from every level—professional, college, high school, amateur, and the Olympics—with photos, memorabilia, and movies covering the history of the game. And there's even an exhibit that enables visitors to play one-on-one—via advanced video technology—against Hall-of-Famer Bill Walton. There's also a "Shoot-Out" in which fans on a moving sidewalk get a chance to shoot baskets at different heights and from varying distances.

As for the honored inductees in the Hall, nominations are made in four categories—player, coach, referee, and contributor. The Honors committee, composed of 24 members representing all levels of basketball, votes each year on the nominees. Eighteen votes are required for election. Players have to be retired for five years before they are eligible.

Seven legends of the game were inducted into the Hall in 1995. They are:

Kareem Abdul-Jabbar: The NBA's all-time leading scorer with 38,387 regular-season points . . . His 5,762 points in the playoffs is also tops in history . . . Only player in NBA history to win six MVP awards . . . Born Lewis Alcindor in New York City on April 16, 1947, he attended UCLA, led the Bruins to three consecutive NCAA championships (1967-69), and was named Most Outstanding Player three times . . . Drafted by Milwaukee Bucks in 1969, the 7'2" giant led the team to its only NBA title in his second season . . . Traded to Los Angeles in 1975, he went on to lead Lakers to five NBA titles between 1980 and 1988 . . . Retired in 1989 after 20 seasons.

Anne Donovan: Dominated women's college basketball at Old Dominion from 1979 to 1983 . . . Born November 1, 1961, in Ridgewood, New Jersey, Donovan grew to 6'8" by the time she attended Old Dominion . . . Led Lady Monarchs to 37-1 record in freshman year and finished college career as 3-time All-American, with averages of 20 points and 14.5 rebounds . . . 3-time Olympian (1980, 1984, 1988) and 2-time gold-medal winner (1984, 1988) for U. S. women's team . . . Played professionally for five years in Japan and one year in Italy.

Vern Mikkelsen: Known as one of the NBA's first power forwards . . . Born October 10, 1928, in Fresno, California, the 6'7" Mikkelsen led Hamline University to the NAIA championship in 1949 . . . Joined the Minneapolis Lakers that autumn and went on to play

10 seasons in NBA . . . A member of four Laker championship teams and six all-star teams . . . Finished career with 10,063 points (14.4 per game) and 5,940 rebounds (8.4) . . . An iron man, he played in 699 of a possible 704 games.

Cheryl Miller: One of the greatest players in the history of women's basketball . . . Born January 3, 1964, in Riverside, California, Miller dominated the game as a 6'3" forward in high school and college . . . Scored 105 points in a high-school game and led her team to 132-4 four-year record . . . Went on to the University of Southern California and was named All-American four times, finishing her career with 3,018 points—second on the women's all-time list . . . Led USC to back-to-back NCAA championships and won tournament MVP award each time . . . A member of the 1984 Olympic gold-medal-winning team . . . Currently coach at USC and does television commentary.

Aleksandr Gomelsky: Known as the father of Soviet men's basketball . . . Coached Soviet Union national team to seven European championships, two World Championships, and the gold medal in the Olympics (1988) . . . Guided Soviets to silver medal in 1964 and bronze medals in 1968 and 1980 . . . Compiled 490-177 record in 29 years of coaching . . . Born January 18, 1928, in Leningrad, Russia . . . In later years he conducted coaching clinics throughout the world and authored 10 books on basketball strategy.

John Kundla: Named coach of the Minneapolis Lakers in 1947, he led team to six titles in his 12-year career, compiling a 466-319 record . . . One of only three coaches in NBA history to win three consecutive championships . . . Born July 3, 1916, in Star Junction, Pennsylvania . . . Played at University of Minnesota and returned there to coach in 1959 after leaving the NBA.

Earl Strom: One of the NBA's most popular referees during his 32-year career . . . Born December 15, 1927, in Pottstown, Pennsylvania, he started calling NBA games in 1957 and earned the nickname "Pied Piper" for his ability to maintain order with his whistle . . . Went on to officiate 2,400 regular-season and 295 playoff games, including 29 in the NBA Finals . . . Officiated Game 7 in five NBA Finals . . . Retired from refereeing in 1990 and died July 10, 1994.

Hall of Fame Electees

Individuals associated with NBA appear in bold type.

*Deceased

PLAYERS

Name	Year Elected
Abdul-Jabbar, Kareem	**1995**
Archibald, Nate	**1991**
Arizin, Paul	**1977**
* Barlow, Thomas "Tarzan"	1980
Barry, Rick	**1986**
Baylor, Elgin	**1976**
* Beckman, John	1973
Bellamy, Walt	**1993**
Belov, Sergei	1992
Bing, Dave	**1990**
Blazejowski, Carol	**1994**
Bradley, Bill	**1982**
* Brennan, Joe	1974
Cervi, Al	**1984**
Chamberlain, Wilt	**1978**
* Cooper, Charles "Tarzan"	1967
Cousy, Bob	**1970**
Cowens, Dave	**1991**
Cuningham, Billy	**1985**
* **Davies, Bob**	**1969**
* DeBernardi, Forrest "Red"	1961
DeBusschere, Dave	**1982**
* Dehnert, Henry "Dutch"	1968
Donovan, Anne	1995
Endacott, Paul	1971
Erving, Julius	**1993**
Foster, Harold "Bud"	1964
Frazier, Walt "Clyde"	**1986**
* Friedman, Max "Marty"	1971
* **Fulks, Joe**	**1977**
Gale, Lauren "Laddie"	1976
Gallatin, Harry	**1991**
Gates, William "Pop"	1988
Gola, Tom	**1975**
Greer, Hal	**1981**
* Gruenig, Robert "Ace"	1963
Hagan, Cliff	**1977**
* Hanson, Victor	1960
Havlicek, John	**1983**
Hawkins, Connie	**1992**
Hayes, Elvin	**1990**
Heinsohn, Tom	**1985**
Holman, Nat	1964
Houbregs, Robert	**1986**
* Hyatt, Charles "Chuck"	1959
Issel, Dan	**1993**
Jeannette, Harry	**1994**
Johnson, William	1976
* **Johnston, Neil**	**1990**
Jones, K.C.	**1988**
Jones, Sam	**1983**
* Krause, Edward "Moose"	1975
Kurland, Bob	1961

Coaches

Gomelsky, Aleksandr 1995
Harshman, Marv 1984
* Hickey, Ed 1978
* Hobson, Howard 1965
**Holzman, William
"Red"** **1985**
* Iba, Henry "Hank" 1968
* **Julian, Alvin
"Doggie"** **1967**
* Keaney, Frank 1960
* Keogan, George 1961
Knight, Bobby 1991
Kundla, John **1995**
* Lambert, Ward
"Piggy" 1960
Litwack, Harry 1975
* Loeffler, Ken 1964
* Lonborg, Arthur
"Dutch" 1972
* McCutchan, Arad 1980
McGuire, Al **1992**
McGuire, Frank **1976**
* Meanwell, Dr. Walter 1959
Meyer, Ray 1978
Miller, Ralph 1987
Ramsay, Jack 1992
Rubini, Cesare 1994
* Rupp, Adolph 1968
* Sachs, Leonard 1961
* Shelton, Everett 1979
Smith, Dean 1982
Taylor, Fred 1985
Wade, Margaret 1984
Watts, Stanley 1985
Wooden, John 1972
* Woolpert, Phil 1992

Contributors

* Abbot, Senda
Berenson 1984
* Allen, Dr. Forrest
"Phog" 1959
* **Bee, Clair** **1967**
* **Brown, Walter** **1965**
* Bunn, John 1964
* Douglas, Robert 1971
* Duer, Alva 1981
Fagan, Clifford 1983
* Fisher, Harry 1973
* **Fleisher, Lawrence** **1991**
* **Gottlieb, Eddie** **1971**
* Gulick, Dr. Luther 1959
Harrison, Lester **1979**
* Hepp, Ferenc 1980
* Hickox, Edward 1959
* Hinkle, Paul "Tony" 1965
* **Irish, Ned** **1964**
* Jones, R. William 1964
* **Kennedy, Walter** **1980**
* Liston, Emil 1974
McLendon, John 1978
* **Mokray, Bill** **1965**
* Morgan, Ralph 1959
* Morgenweck, Frank 1962
* Naismith, Dr. James 1959
Newell, Pete **1978**
* O'Brien, John 1961
* **O'Brien, Lawrence** **1991**
* **Olsen, Harold** **1959**
* **Podoloff, Maurice** **1973**
* Porter, Henry 1960
* Reid, William 1963
* Ripley, Elmer 1972
* St. John, Lynn 1962
* Saperstein, Abe 1970

* Schabinger, Arthur	1961
* Stagg, Amos Alonzo	1959
Stankovic, Boris	1991
* Steitz, Edward	1983
* Taylor, Charles "Chuck"	1968
* Teague, Bertha	1984
* Tower, Oswald	1959
* Trester, Arthur	1961
* Wells, Clifford	1971
* Wilke, Lou	1982

Referees

* Enright, Jim	**1978**
Hepbron, George	1960
* Hoyt, George	1961
* Kennedy, Matthew "Pat"	**1959**
* Leith, Lloyd	1982
Mihalik, Zig "Red"	1985
Nucatola, John	**1977**
* Quigley, Ernest	1961
* Shirley, J. Dallas	**1979**
* Strom, Earl	**1995**
* Tobey, David	1961
* Walsh, David	1961

Teams

First Team	1959
Original Celtics	1959
Buffalo Germans	1961
New York Renaissance	1963

Be a Super Stat Star

The drama is on the court, but basketball fans know there's always a story in the statistics. The daily newspapers provide the basics in box scores, standings, averages, and individual leaders. But some followers of the sport enjoy doing their own stats. Here's how you do it.

Scoring

To get a scoring average, take the player's total points and divide them by the number of games played. For example, if Penny Hardaway has scored 91 points in his first 7 games, divide 91 by 7, which comes to 13 points per game.

QUICK QUIZ

1. Karl Malone has scored 28, 32, and 21 points in his first three games. What is Malone's scoring average?

2. Shaquille O'Neal scored 126 points in his first five games, then scored 42 points in Game 6. What is his average?

3. Robert Horry scored 127 points in the first six games of a playoff series. How many points will he need to score in Game 7 to average 20 points in the series?

See answers on page 230.

Shooting Percentage

To figure out a shooting percentage, take the player's shots made and divide them by the number of shots attempted. For example, if Shawn Kemp has made 9 of 15 shots, you divide 9 by 15, which is .600, or 60 percent.

QUICK QUIZ

1. Over a 3-game span, Grant Hill shot 8-for-14, 6-for-15, and 6-for-9. What is his shooting percentage?

2. If Mitch Richmond makes his first 11 free throws, then misses two of his next three, what is his shooting percentage?

3. If Dana Barros makes all three of his 3-point attempts one night, then goes 2-for-5 the next night, what is his percentage?

See answers on page 230.

Rebounding

To figure out a rebounding average, take the player's total rebounds and divide them by the number of games played. For example, if Patrick Ewing has grabbed 46 rebounds in five games, you divide 46 by 5, which is 9.2 rebounds per game.

QUICK QUIZ

1. If Dennis Rodman has a 4-game stretch with 15, 11, 13, and 16 rebounds, what is his rebounding average?

2. If Hakeem Olajuwon has 32 rebounds in three

games, how many does he need in his next game to average exactly 11?

3. Who has a higher rebound average, Tyrone Hill with 50 rebounds in four games, or Shawn Kemp with 58 rebounds in five games?

See answers on page 230.

Assists

To figure out a player's assist average, take his total assists and divide them by the number of games played. For example, if Tim Hardaway has 84 assists in 12 games, you divide 84 by 12, which is 7.0 assists per game.

QUICK QUIZ

1. If Kenny Anderson starts the season with 11, 8, 10, 7, and 14 assists in five games, what is his assist average?

2. If John Stockton has 97 assists in eight games, how many assists does he need in his next game to average exactly 12?

3. Who has a higher assist average, Tim Hardaway with 31 assists in four games, or Rod Strickland with 28 assists in three games?

See answers on page 230.

Blocked Shots

To figure out a player's blocked-shot average, take his total blocks and divide them by the number of games played. For example, if Dikembe Mutombo has 35 blocks in 15 games, divide 35 by 15, which is 2.33 blocks per game.

QUICK QUIZ

1. If Shawn Bradley has 13 blocks in four games, how many does he need in his next game to average exactly three?

2. If Vlade Divac is credited with 3, 2, 5, 6, 3, and 4 blocks in a 6-game span, what is his blocked-shot average?

3. Who has a higher blocked-shot average, David Robinson with 39 blocks in 16 games, or Alonzo Mourning with 28 blocks in 12 games?

See answers on page 230.

Steals

To figure out a player's average number of steals, take his total steals and divide them by the number of games played. For example, if Eric Murdock has 36 steals in 15 games, you divide 36 by 15, which is 2.40 steals per game.

QUICK QUIZ

1. If Gary Payton has 35 steals in his first 12 games, how many steals does he need in his next game to average exactly three?

2. If Nate McMillan is credited with 4, 3, 1, 3, 2, and 5 steals in a 6-game span, what is his steals average?

3. Who has a higher steals average, Mookie Blaylock

with 17 steals in 6 games, or Jason Kidd with 21 steals in 7 games?

See answers on bottom of page.

ANSWERS TO QUICK QUIZZES

NBA Champions
and Award Winners

No team has ever won as many NBA titles as the Boston Celtics. They have reached the winner's circle 16 times, including 8 in a row in the 1950s and 1960s. The runner-up Los Angeles Lakers have taken the crown six times and, adding their earlier years as a franchise in Minneapolis, the Lakers total 11 championships.

NBA CHAMPIONS

Season	Champion	Eastern Division W.	L.		Western Division W.	L.	
1946-47	Philadelphia	35	25	Philadelphia	39	22	Chicago
1947-48	Baltimore	27	21	Philadelphia	28	20	Baltimore
1948-49	Minneapolis	38	22	Washington	44	16	Minneapolis
1949-50	Minneapolis	51	13	Syracuse	51	17	Minneapolis
1950-51	Rochester	36	30	New York	41	27	Rochester
1951-52	Minneapolis	37	29	New York	40	28	Minneapolis
1952-53	Minneapolis	47	23	New York	48	22	Minneapolis
1953-54	Minneapolis	42	30	Syracuse	46	26	Minneapolis
1954-55	Syracuse	43	29	Syracuse	43	29	Ft. Wayne
1955-56	Philadelphia	45	27	Philadelphia	37	35	Ft. Wayne
1956-57	Boston	44	28	Boston	34	38	St. Louis
1957-58	St. Louis	49	23	Boston	41	31	St. Louis
1958-59	Boston	52	20	Boston	33	39	Minneapolis
1959-60	Boston	59	16	Boston	46	29	St. Louis
1960-61	Boston	57	22	Boston	51	28	St. Louis
1961-62	Boston	60	20	Boston	54	26	Los Angeles
1962-63	Boston	58	22	Boston	53	27	Los Angeles
1963-64	Boston	59	21	Boston	48	32	San Francisco
1964-65	Boston	62	18	Boston	49	31	Los Angeles
1965-66	Boston	54	26	Boston	45	35	Los Angeles
1966-67	Philadelphia	68	13	Philadelphia	44	37	San Francisco
1967-68	Boston	54	28	Boston	52	30	Los Angeles
1968-69	Boston	48	34	Boston	55	27	Los Angeles
1969-70	New York	60	22	New York	46	36	Los Angeles
1970-71	Milwaukee	42	40	Baltimore	66	16	Milwaukee
1971-72	Los Angeles	48	34	New York	69	13	Los Angeles
1972-73	New York	57	25	New York	60	22	Los Angeles
1973-74	Boston	56	26	Boston	59	23	Milwaukee
1974-75	Golden State	60	22	Washington	48	34	Golden State
1975-76	Boston	54	28	Boston	42	40	Phoenix
1976-77	Portland	50	32	Philadelphia	49	33	Portland
1977-78	Washington	44	38	Washington	47	35	Seattle
1978-79	Seattle	54	28	Washington	52	30	Seattle
1979-80	Los Angeles	59	23	Philadelphia	60	22	Los Angeles
1980-81	Boston	62	20	Boston	40	42	Houston
1981-82	Los Angeles	58	24	Philadelphia	57	25	Los Angeles
1982-83	Philadelphia	65	17	Philadelphia	58	24	Los Angeles
1983-84	Boston	62	20	Boston	54	28	Los Angeles
1984-85	L.A. Lakers	63	19	Boston	62	20	L.A. Lakers
1985-86	Boston	67	15	Boston	51	31	Houston
1986-87	L.A. Lakers	59	23	Boston	65	17	L.A. Lakers
1987-88	L.A. Lakers	54	28	Detroit	62	20	L.A. Lakers

1988-89	Detroit	63	19	Detroit	57	25	L.A. Lakers
1989-90	Detroit	59	23	Detroit	59	23	Portland
1990-91	Chicago	61	21	Chicago	58	24	L.A. Lakers
1991-92	Chicago	67	15	Chicago	57	25	Portland
1992-93	Chicago	57	25	Chicago	62	20	Phoenix
1993-94	Houston	57	25	New York	58	24	Houston
1994-95	Houston	57	25	Orlando	47	35	Houston

NBA Scoring Champions

Wilt Chamberlain and Michael Jordan share honors for most scoring titles (7). Wilt did it with the Philadelphia and San Francisco Warriors and the Philadelphia 76ers. Jordan's came as the leader of the 3-time champion Chicago Bulls.

NBA SCORING CHAMPIONS

Season	Pts./Avg.	Top Scorer	Team
1946-47	1389	Joe Fulks	Philadelphia
1947-48	1007	Max Zaslofsky	Chicago
1948-49	1698	George Mikan	Minneapolis
1949-50	1865	George Mikan	Minneapolis
1950-51	1932	George Mikan	Minneapolis
1951-52	1674	Paul Arizin	Philadelphia
1952-53	1564	Neil Johnston	Philadelphia
1953-54	1759	Neil Johnston	Philadelphia
1954-55	1631	Neil Johnston	Philadelphia
1955-56	1849	Bob Pettit	St. Louis
1956-57	1817	Paul Arizin	Philadelphia
1957-58	2001	George Yardley	Detroit
1958-59	2105	Bob Pettit	St. Louis
1959-60	2707	Wilt Chamberlain	Philadelphia
1960-61	3033	Wilt Chamberlain	Philadelphia
1961-62	4029	Wilt Chamberlain	Philadelphia
1962-63	3586	Wilt Chamberlain	San Francisco
1963-64	2948	Wilt Chamberlain	San Francisco
1964-65	2534	Wilt Chamberlain	San Francisco-Philadelphia
1965-66	2649	Wilt Chamberlain	Philadelphia

1966-67	2775	Rick Barry	San Francisco
1967-68	2142	Dave Bing	Detroit
1968-69	2327	Elvin Hayes	San Diego
1969-70	*31.2	Jerry West	Los Angeles
1970-71	*31.7	K. Abdul-Jabbar	Milwaukee
1971-72	*34.8	K. Abdul-Jabbar	Milwaukee
1972-73	*34.0	Nate Archibald	K.C.-Omaha
1973-74	*30.6	Bob McAdoo	Buffalo
1974-75	*34.5	Bob McAdoo	Buffalo
1975-76	*31.1	Bob McAdoo	Buffalo
1976-77	*31.1	Pete Maravich	New Orleans
1977-78	*27.2	George Gervin	San Antonio
1978-79	*29.6	George Gervin	San Antonio
1979-80	*33.1	George Gervin	San Antonio
1980-81	*30.7	Adrian Dantley	Utah
1981-82	*32.3	George Gervin	San Antonio
1982-83	*28.4	Alex English	Denver
1983-84	*30.6	Adrian Dantley	Utah
1984-85	*32.9	Bernard King	New York
1985-86	*30.3	Dominique Wilkins	Atlanta
1986-87	*37.1	Michael Jordan	Chicago
1987-88	*35.0	Michael Jordan	Chicago
1988-89	*32.5	Michael Jordan	Chicago
1989-90	*33.6	Michael Jordan	Chicago
1990-91	*31.2	Michael Jordan	Chicago
1991-92	*30.1	Michael Jordan	Chicago
1992-93	*32.6	Michael Jordan	Chicago
1993-94	*29.8	David Robinson	San Antonio
1994-95	*29.3	Shaquille O'Neal	Orlando

*Scoring title based on best average with at least 70 games played or 1,400 points
1955-56 Bob Pettit, St. Louis

NBA MOST VALUABLE PLAYER

1956-57	Bob Cousy, Boston	1968-69	Wes Unseld, Baltimore
1957-58	Bill Russell, Boston	1969-70	Willis Reed, New York
1958-59	Bob Pettit, St. Louis	1970-71	Kareem Abdul-Jabbar, Milwaukee
1959-60	Wilt Chamberlain, Philadelphia	1971-72	Kareem Abdul-Jabbar, Milwaukee
1960-61	Bill Russell, Boston	1972-73	Dave Cowens
1961-62	Bill Russell, Boston	1973-74	Kareem Abdul-Jabbar, Milwaukee
1962-63	Bill Russell, Boston	1974-75	Bob McAdoo, Buffalo
1963-64	Oscar Robertson, Cincinnati	1975-76	Kareem Abdul-Jabbar, L.A.
1964-65	Bill Russell, Boston	1976-77	Kareem Abdul-Jabbar, L.A.
1965-66	Wilt Chamberlain, Philadelphia	1978-79	Moses Malone, Houston
1967-68	Wilt Chamberlain, Philadelphia	1979-80	Kareem Abdul-Jabbar, L.A.

1980-81	Julius Erving, Philadelphia	1988-89	Magic Johnson, L.A. Lakers
1981-82	Moses Malone, Houston	1989-90	Magic Johnson, L.A. Lakers
1982-83	Moses Malone, Philadelphia	1990-91	Michael Jordan, Chicago
1984-85	Larry Bird, Boston	1991-92	Michael Jordan, Chicago
1985-86	Larry Bird, Boston	1992-93	Charles Barkley, Phoenix
1986-87	Magic Johnson, L.A. Lakers	1993-94	Hakeem Olajuwon, Houston
1987-88	Michael Jordan, Chicago	1994-95	David Robinson, San Antonio

NBA FINALS MVP AWARD

1969	Jerry West, Los Angeles	1983	Moses Malone, Philadelphia
1970	Willis Reed, New York	1984	Larry Bird, Boston
1971	Kareem Abdul-Jabbar, Milwaukee	1985	Kareem Abdul-Jabbar, L.A. Lakers
1972	Wilt Chamberlain, Los Angeles		
1973	Willis Reed, New York	1986	Larry Bird, Boston
1974	John Havlicek, Boston	1987	Magic Johnson, L.A. Lakers
1975	Rick Barry, Golden State	1988	James Worthy, L.A. Lakers
1976	Jo Jo White, Boston	1989	Joe Dumars, Detroit
1977	Bill Walton, Portland	1990	Isiah Thomas, Detroit
1978	Wes Unseld, Washington	1991	Michael Jordan, Chicago
1979	Dennis Johnson, Seattle	1992	Michael Jordan, Chicago
1980	Magic Johnson, Los Angeles	1993	Michael Jordan, Chicago
1981	Cedric Maxwell, Boston	1994	Hakeem Olajuwon, Houston
1982	Magic Johnson, Los Angeles	1995	Hakeem Olajuwon, Houston

SCHICK NBA ROOKIE OF THE YEAR

1947-48	Paul Hoffman, Baltimore	1963-64	Jerry Lucas, Cincinnati
1948-49	Howie Shannon, Providence	1964-65	Willis Reed, New York
1949-50	Alex Groza, Indianapolis	1965-66	Rick Barry, San Francisco
1950-51	Paul Arizin, Philadelphia	1966-67	Dave Bing, Detroit
1951-52	Bill Tosheff, Indianapolis	1967-68	Earl Monroe, Baltimore
	Mel Hutchins, Milwaukee	1968-69	Wes Unseld, Baltimore
1952-53	Don Meineke, Fort Wayne	1969-70	Kareem Abdul-Jabbar, Milwaukee
1953-54	Ray Felix, Baltimore		
1954-55	Bob Pettit, Milwaukee	1970-71	Dave Cowens, Boston
1955-56	Maurice Stokes, Rochester		Geoff Petrie, Portland
1956-57	Tom Heinsohn, Boston	1971-72	Sidney Wicks, Portland
1957-58	Woody Sauldsberry, Philadelphia	1972-73	Bob McAdoo, Buffalo
1958-59	Elgin Baylor, Minneapolis	1973-74	Ernie DiGregorio, Buffalo
1959-60	Wilt Chamberlain, Philadelphia	1974-75	Keith Wilkes, Golden State.
1960-61	Oscar Robertson, Cincinnati	1976-77	Adrian Dantley, Buffalo
1961-62	Walt Bellamy, Chicago	1977-78	Walter Davis, Phoenix
1962-63	Terry Dischinger, Chicago	1978-79	Phil Ford, Kansas City

1979-80 Larry Bird, Boston	1988-89 Mitch Richmond, Golden State
1980-81 Darrell Griffith, Utah	1989-90 David Robinson, San Antonio
1981-82 Buck Williams, New Jersey	1990-91 Derrick Coleman, New Jersey
1982-83 Terry Cummings, San Diego	1991-92 Larry Johnson, Charlotte
1983-84 Ralph Sampson, Houston	1992-93 Shaquille O'Neal, Orlando
1984-85 Michael Jordan, Chicago	1993-94 Chris Webber, Golden State
1985-86 Patrick Ewing, New York	1994-95 Grant Hill, Detroit
1986-87 Chuck Person, Indiana	Jason Kidd, Dallas
1987-88 Mark Jackson, New York	

NBA DEFENSIVE PLAYER OF THE YEAR

1982-83 Sidney Moncrief, Milwaukee	1989-90 Dennis Rodman, Detroit
1983-84 Sidney Moncrief, Milwaukee	1990-91 Dennis Rodman, Detroi
1984-85 Mark Eaton, Utah	1991-92 David Robinson,t
1985-86 Alvin Robertson, San Antonio	San Antonio
1986-87 Michael Cooper, L.A. Lakers	1992-93 Hakeem Olajuwon, Houston
1987-88 Michael Jordan, Chicago	1993-94 Hakeem Olajuwon, Houston
1988-89 Mark Eaton, Utah	1994-95 Dikembe Mutombo, Denver

NBA SIXTH MAN AWARD

1982-83 Bobby Jones, Philadelphia	1989-90 Ricky Pierce, Milwaukee
1983-84 Kevin McHale, Boston	1990-91 Detlef Schrempf, Indiana
1984-85 Kevin McHale, Boston	1991-92 Detlef Schrempf, Indiana
1985-86 Bill Walton, Boston	1992-93 Cliff Robinson, Portland
1986-87 Ricky Pierce, Milwaukee	1993-94 Dell Curry, Charlotte
1987-88 Roy Tarpley, Dallas	1994-95 Anthony Mason, New York
1988-89 Eddie Johnson, Phoenix	

NBA MOST IMPROVED PLAYER

1985-86 Alvin Robertson, San Antonio	1990-91 Scott Skiles, Orlando
1986-87 Dale Ellis, Seattle	1991-92 Pervis Ellison, Washington
1987-88 Kevin Duckworth, Portland	1992-93 Chris Jackson, Denver
1988-89 Kevin Johnson, Phoenix	1993-94 Don MacLean, Washington
1989-90 Rony Seikaly, Miami	1994-95 Dana Barros, Philadelphia

IBM AWARD
Determined by Computer Formula

1983-84 Magic Johnson, Los Angeles	1989-90 David Robinson, San Antonio
1984-85 Michael Jordan, Chicago	1990-91 David Robinson, San Antonio
1985-86 Charles Barkley, Philadelphia	1991-92 Dennis Rodman, Detroit
1986-87 Charles Barkley, Philadelphia	1992-93 Hakeem Olajuwon, Houston
1987-88 Charles Barkley, Philadelphia	1993-94 David Robinson, San Antonio
1988-89 Michael Jordan, Chicago	1994-95 David Robinson, San Antonio

IBM NBA COACH OF THE YEAR

1962-63 Harry Gallatin, St. Louis
1963-64 Alex Hannum, San Francisco
1964-65 Red Auerbach, Boston
1965-66 Dolph Schayes, Philadelphia
1966-67 Johnny Kerr, Chicago
1967-68 Richie Guerin, St. Louis
1968-69 Gene Shue, Baltimore
1969-70 Red Holzman, New York
1970-71 Dick Motta, Chicago
1971-72 Bill Sharman, Los Angeles
1972-73 Tom Heinsohn, Boston
1973-74 Ray Scott, Detroit
1974-75 Phil Johnson,
        Kansas City-Omaha
1975-76 Bill Fitch, Cleveland
1976-77 Tom Nissalke, Houston
1977-78 Hubie Brown, Atlanta
1978-79 Cotton Fitzsimmons, Kansas City

1979-80 Bill Fitch, Boston
1980-81 Jack McKinney, Indiana
1981-82 Gene Shue, Washington
1982-83 Don Nelson, Milwaukee
1983-84 Frank Layden, Utah
1984-85 Don Nelson, Milwaukee
1985-86 Mike Fratello, Atlanta
1986-87 Mike Schuler, Portland
1987-88 Doug Moe, Denver
1988-89 Cotton Fitzsimmons,
        Phoenix
1989-90 Pat Riley, L.A. Lakers
1990-91 Don Chaney, Houston
1991-92 Don Nelson, Golden State
1992-93 Pat Riley, New York
1993-94 Lenny Wilkens, Atlanta
1994-95 Del Harris, L.A. Lakers

J. WALTER KENNEDY CITIZENSHIP AWARD

1974-75 Wes Unseld, Washington
1975-76 Slick Watts, Seattle
1976-77 Dave Bing, Washington
1977-78 Bob Lanier, Detroit
1978-79 Calvin Murphy, Houston
1979-80 Austin Carr, Cleveland
1980-81 Mike Glenn, New York
1981-82 Kent Benson, Detroit
1982-83 Julius Erving, Philadelphia
1983-84 Frank Layden, Utah
1984-85 Dan Issel, Denver

1985-86 Michael Cooper, L.A. Lakers
        Rory Sparrow, New York
1986-87 Isiah Thomas, Detroit
1987-88 Alex English, Denver
1988-89 Thurl Bailey, Utah
1989-90 Glenn Rivers, Atlanta
1990-91 Kevin Johnson, Phoenix
1991-92 Magic Johnson, L.A. Lakers
1992-93 Terry Porter, Portland
1993-94 Joe Dumars, Detroit
1994-95 Joe O'Toole, Atlanta

The NBA Record Book

— — —

Some NBA records will live forever. Others are in danger of being broken this season and in the future. Here's a look at some super stats, amazing achievements, NBA Top 10s, and records that have made sports history.

Most Games Played

He started his career when Richard Nixon was president and ended it with George Bush. In the long history of the NBA, no one has played more games than Kareem Abdul-Jabbar, who came into the league as Lew Alcindor in 1969 and proceeded to rewrite the NBA record book.

The main challenge to Abdul-Jabbar has come from Robert Parish, who at the age of 42 was starting his 19th NBA season in 1995-96.

Kareem Abdul-Jabbar	1,560
Robert Parish	1,494
Moses Malone	1,329
Elvin Hayes	1,303
John Havlicek	1,270
Paul Silas	1,254
Alex English	1,193
Tree Rollins	1,156
Hal Greer	1,122
Buck Williams	1,122

Most Points

Can anyone ever overtake Kareem Abdul-Jabbar and become the league's all-time scorer? It appeared Michael Jordan might have the best chance before he took off nearly two seasons to pursue a career in baseball. Jordan returned late in the 1994–95 season and should crack the Top 10 list soon, but it seems his chance of catching Kareem is gone.

San Antonio's David Robinson and Orlando's Shaquille O'Neal, who battled for the scoring title in both 1994 and 1995, are considered the best bets to someday make the leader board.

Kareem Abdul-Jabbar	38,387
Wilt Chamberlain	31,419
Moses Malone	27,409
Elvin Hayes	27,313
Oscar Robertson	26,710
John Havlicek	26,395
Alex English	25,613
Dominique Wilkins	25,389
Jerry West	25,192
Adrian Dantley	23,177

Most Points in a Game

Only two active players, San Antonio's David Robinson and Chicago's Michael Jordan, are among the Top 10 all-time single-game scorers. Jordan scored 69 points against the Cleveland Caveliers in 1990 and Robinson netted 71 points against the Los Angeles Clippers on the final day of the 1993–94 regular season. Glen Rice had the most prolific day by an NBA player in 1994–95 when he torched the Orlando Magic for 56 points on April 15, 1995.

Wilt Chamberlain dominates this list, having scored 70 or more points six times in his brilliant career.

Wilt Chamberlain	100	Philadelphia vs. New York, March 2, 1962
Wilt Chamberlain	78	Philadelphia vs. Los Angeles (3 OT), Dec. 8, 1961
Wilt Chamberlain	73	Philadelphia vs. Chicago, Jan. 13, 1962
Wilt Chamberlain	73	San Francisco vs. New York, Nov. 16, 1962
David Thompson	73	Denver vs. Detroit, April 9, 1978
Wilt Chamberlain	72	San Francisco vs. Los Angeles, Nov. 3, 1962
Elgin Baylor	71	Los Angeles vs. New York, Nov. 15, 1960
David Robinson	71	San Antonio vs. L.A. Clippers, April 24, 1994
Wilt Chamberlain	70	San Francisco vs. Syracuse, March 10, 1963
Michael Jordan	69	Chicago vs. Cleveland, March 28, 1990

Highest Scoring Average
(Minimum 400 Games or 10,000 Points)

Michael Jordan's nickname is "Air," but it might as well be "Rare." For rarely has a player come into the NBA and dominated it the way Jordan has since 1984. He tied Wilt Chamberlain's record of seven straight scoring championships, the streak ending only when Michael decided to "retire" in 1993. He came back late in the 1994–95 season and once again established himself as one of the game's greatest scorers.

	Games	Points	Average
Michael Jordan	684	21,998	32.2
Wilt Chamberlain	1,045	31,419	30.1
Elgin Baylor	846	23,149	27.4
Jerry West	932	25,192	27.0
Bob Pettit	792	20,880	26.4
George Gervin	791	20,708	26.2
Karl Malone	816	21,237	26.0
Dominique Wilkins	984	25,389	25.8
David Robinson	475	12,209	25.7
Oscar Robertson	1,040	26,710	25.7

Most Field Goals Made

The Orlando Magic's most basic play goes like this: Penny Hardaway brings the ball upcourt, finds Shaquille O'Neal on the low post, and Shaq overpowers his defender for an easy dunk. The play has been so effective in recent years that O'Neal led the NBA in field goals in both 1993–94 and 1994–95. His 930 field goals in the latter season were 100 more than any other player.

Shaq would have to average 900 field goals per season for 17 seasons to catch Kareem Abdul-Jabbar, who set an almost unreachable record with 15,837 field goals.

Kareem Abdul-Jabbar	15,837
Wilt Chamberlain	12,681
Elvin Hayes	10,976
Alex English	10,659
John Havlicek	10,513
Dominique Wilkins	9,516
Oscar Robertson	9,508
Moses Malone	9,435
Robert Parish	9,424
Jerry West	9,016

Most Field Goals Attempted

This is one category that will likely be forever dominated by old-time players. The reason is simple: Teams in the 1960s and 1970s used to average over 100 attempts per game, while modern-day teams are usually in the 80-to-85 range. Stars in the 1960s would routinely attempt 2,300 shots per season but few players today approach the 1,800 mark.

In 1994–95, for example, Shaquille O'Neal led the NBA with 1,594 field-goal attempts. In comparison, Wilt Chamberlain took 3,159 shots in 1961-62.

Kareem Abdul-Jabbar	28,307
Elvin Hayes	24,272
John Havlicek	23,930
Wilt Chamberlain	23,497
Alex English	21,036
Dominique Wilkins	20,504
Elgin Baylor	20,171
Oscar Robertson	19,620
Moses Malone	19,225
Jerry West	19,032

Highest Field-Goal Percentage
(2,000 Field Goals Made Minimum)

It's the best approach to an almost automatic two points: find the center close to the basket and feed him. So it's no surprise that the majority of the NBA's all-time leaders in field-goal percentage are centers.

Chris Gatling of the Golden State Warriors led the NBA in 1994–95 with a .633 percentage, the highest in the league since another center, James Donaldson of the Los Angeles Clippers, converted at a .637 rate in 1984–85. Gatling does not have enough baskets to qualify for the all-time Top 10, but there are several active players on the list.

	Field Goals Made	Field Goals Attempted	Percentage
Artis Gilmore	5,732	9,570	.599
Mark West	2,330	3,958	.589
Shaquille O'Neal	2,616	4,489	.583
Steve Johnson	2,841	4,965	.572
Darryl Dawkins	3,477	6,079	.572
James Donaldson	3,105	5,442	.571
Jeff Ruland	2,105	3,734	.564
Kareem Abdul-Jabbar	15,837	28,307	.559
Otis Thorpe	5,283	9,515	.555
Charles Barkley	6,813	12,285	.555

Most Free Throws Made

To make this Top 10 list, a player must have played a long time in the league and also have been a good free-throw shooter. Moses Malone qualifies on both counts. Malone is the all-time leader in this category, thanks mainly to his success rate of better than 76 percent.

Among current players, Karl Malone of Utah is closing in rapidly on this list of leaders. Entering the 1995–96 season, "The Mailman" had converted 5,472 free-throw opportunities.

Moses Malone	8,531
Oscar Robertson	7,694
Jerry West	7,160
Dolph Schayes	6,979
Adrian Dantley	6,832
Kareem Abdul-Jabbar	6,712
Bob Pettit	6,182
Wilt Chamberlain	6,057
Elgin Baylor	5,763
Dominique Wilkins	5,721

Most Free Throws Attempted

Figure that the average player takes about eight seconds to release a foul shot and Wilt Chamberlain took 11,862 shots during his 14-year career. That means he spent the equivalent of 33 full games at the foul line. And, yes, nobody took more free throws.

Special mention should go to Oscar Robertson and Jerry West, the only two guards to make the Top 10 in free throws attempted. Both were not only superb outside shooters but dangerous on the drive, too, forcing defenses into fouls.

Wilt Chamberlain	11,862
Moses Malone	11,090
Kareem Abdul-Jabbar	9,304
Oscar Robertson	9,185
Jerry West	8,801
Adrian Dantley	8,351
Dolph Schayes	8,273
Bob Pettit	8,119
Walt Bellamy	8,088
Elvin Hayes	7,999

Highest Free-Throw Percentage
(Minimum 1,200 Free Throws Made)

Through good times and bad in the NBA's recent history, there has been one constant: Washington's Mark Price clicking at the foul line. Going into the 1995–96 season, the ex-Cavalier guard had converted better than 90 percent of his free-throw attempts.

While Price is the greatest overhanded free-throw shooter in history, a special mention must go to Rick Barry, who converted 90 percent of his free throws while shooting underhanded.

	Free Throws Made	Free Throws Attempted	Percentage
Mark Price	1,883	2,078	.906
Rick Barry	3,818	4,243	.900
Calvin Murphy	3,445	3,864	.892
Scott Skiles	1,540	1,731	.890
Larry Bird	3,960	4,471	.886
Bill Sharman	3,143	3,559	.883
Reggie Miller	3,186	3,624	.879
Ricky Pierce	3,033	3,459	.877
Kiki Vandeweghe	3,484	3,997	.872
Jeff Malone	2,918	3,351	.871

Most 3-Point Field Goals Made

In the 1994-95 playoffs, the Orlando Magic thought they had the right plan to stop the Houston Rockets: double- and triple-team Hakeem Olajuwon when he got the ball down low and hope the Rockets couldn't hit their outside shots if Olajuwon elected to pass the ball back outside. The plan backfired. When Olajuwon couldn't get off a shot, he simply returned the pass to someone open on the perimeter, whether it was Kenny Smith, Robert Horry, or Sam Cassell. The Rockets' 3-point accuracy helped them overcome a 20-point lead in Game 1 of the Finals and then bury the Magic three more times, giving Houston its second straight championship.

No Rocket on the 1995–96 roster is in the Top 10 in all-time 3-pointers made, but it seems only a matter of time before Smith enters the category.

Dale Ellis	1,119
Reggie Miller	1,035
Danny Ainge	1,002
Michael Adams	935
Chuck Person	856
Mark Price	802
Derek Harper	787
Vernon Maxwell	777
Terry Porter	766
Dan Majerle	721

Most 3-Point Field Goals Attempted

In Game 7 of the 1994 NBA Finals, John Starks shot a miserable 2-for-18 as the New York Knicks saw their dreams of a championship ended by the Houston Rockets. Did Starks get discouraged and stop shooting? On the contrary. Starks came out in 1994–95 and set NBA records for 3-point field goals made (217) and attempted (611).

Starks' long-range bombarding wasn't enough to get him on the NBA's all-time list for 3-pointers attempted, but a few more seasons like that and he'll be right there.

Michael Adams	2,816
Dale Ellis	2,783
Danny Ainge	2,651
Reggie Miller	2,622
Vernon Maxwell	2,422
Chuck Person	2,379
Derek Harper	2,244
Terry Porter	2,006
Dominique Wilkins	1,973
Dan Majerle	1,965

Highest 3-Point
Field Goal Percentage

There seems to be little doubt that the 3-point shot has had a marked effect on the NBA. In the last three Finals series, in fact, the 3-pointer has been a crucial weapon. In 1993 John Paxson's 3-pointer in the final seconds gave Chicago its second straight championship. In 1994 Sam Cassell's long 3-pointer lifted Houston to a key victory over the Knicks in Game 3, and the Rockets went on to win the title. Then, in the 1995 Finals, Cassell, Kenny Smith, and Robert Horry rained 3-pointers on the Orlando Magic in a 4-game sweep.

Entering the 1995–96 season, the Chicago Bulls' Steve Kerr is on top of the NBA all-time list in 3-point percentage.

	FGM	FGA	Pct.
Steve Kerr	288	617	.467
B.J. Armstrong	284	650	.437
Drazen Petrovic	255	583	.437
Hubert Davis	190	439	.433
Dana Barros	606	1,453	.417
Mark Price	802	1,960	.409
Trent Tucker	575	1,410	.408
Mike Iuzzolino	113	280	.404
Dale Ellis	1,119	2,783	.402
Hersey Hawkins	685	1,705	.402

Most Rebounds

Dennis Rodman is well-known for his multicolored hair. But ask NBA coaches what they remember most about Rodman and they'll say one word: rebounding. Entering the 1995–96 season, Rodman had led the league in rebounding four straight seasons. Only Moses Malone and Wilt Chamberlain ever won four consecutive rebounding titles. Still, Rodman's career total of 8,489 rebounds is not enough to place him among the NBA's all-time Top 10.

Wilt Chamberlain	23,924
Bill Russell	21,620
Kareem Abdul-Jabbar	17,440
Elvin Hayes	16,279
Moses Malone	16,212
Nate Thurmond	14,464
Robert Parish	14,323
Walt Bellamy	14,241
Wes Unseld	13,769
Jerry Lucas	12,942

Most Assists

Magic Johnson knew it would happen. When the former Los Angeles Lakers superstar retired in 1991, he predicted that John Stockton of the Utah Jazz would someday break Johnson's all-time record for assists. It happened midway through the 1994–95 season when Stockton registered his 9,922nd career assist. The former Gonzaga standout went on to post his seventh season with more than 1,000 assists and extend his career record to 10,394. And there's no end in sight.

John Stockton	10,394
Magic Johnson	9,921
Oscar Robertson	9,887
Isiah Thomas	9,061
Maurice Cheeks	7,392
Lenny Wilkens	7,211
Bob Cousy	6,955
Guy Rodgers	6,917
Nate Archibald	6,476
John Lucas	6,454

Most Personal Fouls

It is not necessarily a bad sign if a person makes the Top 10 in this department. For one thing, a player has to be in the league for quite a few years to draw so many fouls. And being on this list also demonstrates that these players were at least close enough to their man to be charged with a foul. So Robert Parish of the Hornets should feel no shame in getting close to all-time leader Kareem Abdul-Jabbar in this department.

Kareem Abdul-Jabbar	4,657
Robert Parish	4,323
Elvin Hayes	4,193
James Edwards	4,080
Jack Sikma	3,879
Hal Greer	3,855
Buck Williams	3,783
Dolph Schayes	3,664
Bill Laimbeer	3,633
Walt Bellamy	3,536

Most Disqualifications

Shawn Bradley is not only one of the tallest (7'6") players in the NBA; he's also one of the most aggressive on defense. The Philadelphia 76ers center uses his long arms to swat aside shots and deter opponents from driving inside. Unfortunately, those long arms also lead to a lot of foul calls. In 1994–95, Bradley was disqualified due to fouls an NBA-high 18 times.

Bradley, now in his third season, still has a long way to go to catch former Laker Vern Mikkelsen, who was disqualified 127 times in his 10-year Hall of Fame career that spanned the 1950s. (In the NBA, a player who gets six fouls in a game is disqualified.)

Vern Mikkelsen	127
Walter Dukes	121
Charlie Share	105
Paul Arizin	101
Darryl Dawkins	100
James Edwards	96
Tom Sanders	94
Tom Gola	94
Steve Johnson	93
Tree Rollins	92

Most Steals

Few things are more demoralizing to a team than to have the ball stolen. Many times it leads to a 4-point swing, and in a lot of NBA games that swing can mean the difference between winning and losing. Scottie Pippen led the NBA in 1994–95 with 232 steals and has had 1,405 in his first eight seasons in the league. Another year like 1994–95 and Scottie will enter the Top 10 list for career steals.

All-time assists leader John Stockton should assume No. 1 in this category before the 1995–96 season is over. The Jazz guard entered the season only 85 behind all-time leader Maurice Cheeks.

Maurice Cheeks	2,310
John Stockton	2,225
Alvin Robertson	1,946
Isiah Thomas	1,861
Clyde Drexler	1,856
Michael Jordan	1,845
Magic Johnson	1,698
Lafayette Lever	1,666
Gus Williams	1,638
Hakeem Olajuwon	1,581

Most Blocked Shots

Watch your back, Kareem. Yes, Kareem Abdul-Jabbar leads this category, as he does so many others, but Hakeem Olajuwon is gaining rapidly and could overtake him before the end of the 1995–96 season. Olajuwon finished second to Denver's Dikembe Mutombo in blocked-shot average in 1994–95 and entered the new season only 206 behind Abdul-Jabbar.

Mutombo is not yet on the list, but he averaged 288 blocks per year in his first four seasons. If he keeps up this pace, Mutombo will earn a spot on the list around 1999.

Kareem Abdul-Jabbar	3,189
Mark Eaton	3,064
Hakeem Olajuwon	2,983
Tree Rollins	2,542
Robert Parish	2,288
Patrick Ewing	2,143
Manute Bol	2,086
George T. Johnson	2,082
Larry Nance	2,027
Elvin Hayes	1,771

All-Time Winningest Coaches
(Prior to 1995-96 Season)

The 1994–95 season was not a good one for former Celtics boss Red Auerbach, as his record of 938 coaching victories, once thought untouchable, was surpassed by the Atlanta Hawks' Lenny Wilkens. And it's possible that the Dallas Mavericks' Dick Motta will pass Auerbach and move into second place on the all-time list in 1995–96.

Lenny Wilkens	968
Rcd Auerbach	938
Dick Motta	892
Jack Ramsay	864
Bill Fitch	862
Don Nelson	817
Cotton Fitzsimmons	805
Gene Shue	784
Pat Riley	756
John MacLeod	707

All-Time Coaches Winning Percentage
(Minimum 400 Games)

When Pat Riley left the Knicks at the end of the 1994–95 season, the team lost the coach with the highest winning percentage in NBA history. Riley and the Chicago Bulls' Phil Jackson had entered 1994–95 virtually tied for the all-time lead at 72 percent, but Riley's Knicks won 55 games while the Bulls won only 47, giving Riley sole possession of the top spot.

Jerry Sloan was a newcomer to the Top 10 in 1994–95. By guiding the Utah Jazz to a 60–22 record, Sloan extended his career winning percentage to .593, good for tenth place.

	Won	Lost	Pct.
Pat Riley	756	299	.717
Billy Cunningham	454	196	.698
Phil Jackson	342	150	.695
K.C. Jones	522	252	.674
Red Auerbach	938	479	.662
Rick Adelman	291	154	.654
Lester Harrison	295	181	.620
Tom Heinsohn	427	263	.619
Chuck Daly	564	379	.598
Jerry Sloan	458	314	.593

All-Time NBA
Regular Season Records

— — —

Individual
Single Game
Most Points: 100, Wilt Chamberlain, Philadelphia, vs. New York, at Hershey, PA, March 2, 1962

Most FG Attempted: 63, Wilt Chamberlain, Philadelphia, vs. New York, at Hershey, PA, March 2, 1962

Most FG Made: 36, Wilt Chamberlain, Philadelphia, vs. New York, at Hershey, PA, March 2, 1962

Most Consecutive FT Made: 19, Bob Pettit, St. Louis, vs. Boston at Boston, November 22, 1961; Bill Cartright, New York, vs. Kansas City, at NY, November 17, 1981; Adrian Dantley, Detroit, vs. Chicago, at Chicago, December 15, 1987 (OT)

Most FT Missed: 22, Wilt Chamberlain, Philadelphia, vs. Seattle, at Boston, December 1, 1967

Most Rebounds: 55, Wilt Chamberlain, Philadelphia, vs. Boston, November 24, 1960

Most 3-Point FG Attempted: 20, Michael Adams, Denver, vs. L.A. Clippers, at Los Angeles, April 12, 1991

Most 3-Point FG Made: 10, Brian Shaw, Miami, at Milwaukee, April 8, 1993; Joe Dumars, Detroit, vs. Minnesota, at Detroit, November 8, 1994

Most FT Attempted: 34, Wilt Chamberlain, Philadelphia, vs. St. Louis, at Philadelphia, February 22, 1962

Most FT Made: 28, Wilt Chamberlain, Philadelphia, vs. New York, at Hershey, PA, March 2, 1962; Adrian Dantley, Utah, vs. Houston, at Las Vegas, NV, January 4, 1984

Most Consecutive FG Made: 18, Wilt Chamberlain, San Francisco, vs. New York, at Boston, November 27, 1963; Wilt Chamberlain, Philadelphia, vs. Baltimore, at Pittsburgh, February 24, 1967

Most Assists: 30, Scott Skiles, Orlando, vs. Denver, at Orlando, December 30, 1990

Most Blocked Shots: 17, Elmore Smith, Los Angeles, vs. Portland, at Los Angeles, October 28, 1973

Most Steals: 11, Larry Kenon, San Antonio, at Kansas City, December 26, 1976

Most Personal Fouls: 8, Don Otten, Tri-Cities, at Sheboygan, November 24, 1949

Season

Most Points: 4,029, Wilt Chamberlain, Philadelphia, 1961-62

Highest Average: 50.4, Wilt Chamberlain, Philadelphia, 1961-62

Most FG Attempted: 3,159, Wilt Chamberlain, Philadelphia, 1961-62

Most FG Made: 1,597, Wilt Chamberlain, Philadelphia, 1961-62

Highest FG Percentage: .727, Wilt Chamberlain, Los Angeles, 1972-73

Most 3-Point FG Attempted: 611, John Starks, New York, 1994-95

Most 3-Point FG Made: 217, John Starks, New York, 1994-95

Most FT Attempted: 1,363, Wilt Chamberlain, Philadelphia, 1961-62

Most FT Made: 840, Jerry West, Los Angeles, 1965-66

Highest FT Percentage: .958, Calvin Murphy, Houston, 1980-81

Most Rebounds: 2,149, Wilt Chamberlain, Philadelphia, 1960-61

Most Assists: 1,164, John Stockton, Utah, 1990-91

Most Blocked Shots: 456, Mark Eaton, Utah, 1984-85

Most Steals: 301, Alvin Robertson, San Antonio, 1985-86

Most Personal Fouls: 386, Darryl Dawkins, New Jersey, 1983-84

Most Disqualifications: 26, Don Meineke, Fort Wayne, 1952-53

Career

Most Games: 1,560, Kareem Abdul-Jabbar, Milwaukee and Los Angeles Lakers, 1969-89

Most Minutes: 57,446, Kareem Abdul-Jabbar, Milwaukee and Los Angeles Lakers, 1969-89

Most Points Scored: 38,387, Kareem Abdul-Jabbar, Milwaukee and Los Angeles Lakers, 1969-89

Highest Scoring Average: 32.2, Michael Jordan, Chicago, 1984-95

Most FG Attempted: 28,307, Kareem Abdul-Jabbar, Milwaukee and Los Angeles Lakers, 1969-89

Most FG Made: 15,837, Kareem Abdul-Jabbar, Milwaukee and Los Angeles Lakers, 1969-89

Highest FG Percentage: .599, Artis Gilmore, Chicago, San Antonio, and Boston, 1976-88

Most 3-Point FG Attempted: 2,816, Michael Adams, Sacramento, Denver, and Washington, 1985-95

Most 3-Point FG Made: 1,119, Dale Ellis, Dallas, Seattle, Milwaukee, and San Antonio, 1983-95

Most FT Attempted: 11,862, Wilt Chamberlain, Philadelphia, San Francisco, and Los Angeles 1959-73

Most FT Made: 8,531, Moses Malone, Buffalo, Houston, Philadelphia, Washington, Atlanta, Milwaukee, and San Antonio, 1976-95

Highest FT Percentage: .906, Mark Price, Cleveland, 1986-95

Most Rebounds: 23,924, Wilt Chamberlain, Philadelphia, San Francisco, and Los Angeles, 1959-73

Most Assists: 10,394, John Stockton, Utah, 1984-95

Most Blocked Shots: 3,189, Kareem Abdul-Jabbar, Milwaukee and Los Angeles Lakers, 1969-89

Most Steals: 2,310, Maurice Cheeks, Philadelphia, San Antonio, New York, Atlanta, and New Jersey, 1978-93

Most Personal Fouls: 4,657, Kareem Abdul-Jabbar, Milwaukee and Los Angeles Lakers, 1969-89

Most Disqualifications: 127, Vern Mikkelsen, Minneapolis, 1950-59

Team Records

Single Game

Most Points, One Team: 173, Boston, vs. Minneapolis at Boston, February 27, 1959; Phoenix, vs. Denver at Phoenix, November 10, 1990; 186, Detroit, at Denver, December 13, 1983 (3 overtimes)

Most Points, Two Teams: 320, Golden State 162 at Denver 158, November 2, 1990; 370, Detroit 186 at Denver 184, December 13, 1983 (3 overtimes)

Most FG Attempted, One Team: 153, Philadelphia, vs. Los Angeles at Philadelphia, December 8, 1961 (3 overtimes); 150, Boston, vs. Philadelphia at Philadelphia, March 2, 1960

Most FG Attempted, Two Teams: 291, Philadelphia 153 vs. Los Angeles 138 at Philadelphia, December 8, 1961 (3 overtimes); 274, Boston 149 vs. Detroit 125 at Boston, January 27, 1961; Philadelphia 141 vs. Boston 133 at Boston, March 5, 1961

Most FG Made, One Team: 72, Boston, vs. Minneapolis at Boston, February 27, 1959; 74, Denver, vs. Detroit at Denver, December 13, 1983 (3 overtimes)

Most FG Made, Two Teams: 142, Detroit 74 at Denver 68, December 13, 1983 (3 overtimes); 134, San Diego 67 at Cincinnati 67, March 12, 1970

Most FT Attempted, One Team: 86, Syracuse, vs. Anderson at Syracuse, November 24, 1949 (5 overtimes); 71, Chicago, vs. Phoenix at Chicago, January 8, 1970

Most FT Attempted, Two Teams: 160, Syracuse 86 vs. Anderson 74, at Syracuse, November 24, 1949 (5 overtimes); 127, Ft. Wayne 67 vs. Minneapolis 60, at Fort Wayne, December 31, 1954

Most FT Made, One Team: 61, Phoenix, vs. Utah at Phoenix, April 4, 1990 (overtime); 60, Washington, vs. New York at New York, November 13, 1987

Most FT Made, Two Teams: 116, Syracuse 59 vs. Anderson

57, at Syracuse, November 24, 1949 (5 overtimes); 103, Boston 56 at Minneapolis 47, November 28, 1954

Most Rebounds, One Team: 109, Boston, vs. Detroit at Boston, December 24, 1960

Most Rebounds, Two Teams: 188, Philadelphia 98 vs. Los Angeles 90, at Philadelphia, December 8, 1961 (3 overtimes); 177, Philadelphia 104 vs. Syracuse 73 at Philadelphia, November 4, 1959; Boston 89 vs. Philadelphia 88 at Philadelphia, December 27, 1960

Most Assists, One Team: 53, Milwaukee, at Detroit, December 26, 1978

Most Assists, Two Teams: 88, Phoenix 47 vs. San Diego 41, at Tucson, Arizona, March 15, 1969; San Antonio 50 vs. Denver 38 at San Antonio, April 15, 1984; 93, Detroit 47 at Denver 46, December 13, 1983 (3 overtimes)

Most Blocked Shots, One Team: 22, New Jersey, vs. Denver, December 12, 1991

Most Blocked Shots, Two Teams: 34, Detroit 19 vs. Washington 15 at Washington, November 19, 1981

Most Steals, One Team: 25, Golden State, vs. Los Angeles, March 25, 1975; Golden State, vs. San Antonio, February 15, 1989

Most Steals, Two Teams: 40, Golden State 24 vs. Los Angeles 16, January 21, 1975; Philadelphia 24 vs. Detroit 16, November 11, 1978; Golden State 25 vs. San Antonio 15, February 15, 1989

Most Personal Fouls, One Team: 66, Anderson, at Syracuse, November 24, 1949 (5 overtimes); 55, Milwaukee, at Baltimore, November 12, 1952

Most Personal Fouls, Two Teams: 122, Anderson 66 at Syracuse 56, November 24, 1949 (5 overtimes); 97, Syracuse 50 vs. New York 47 at Syracuse, February 15, 1953

Most Disqualifications, One Team: 8, Syracuse, vs. Baltimore at Syracuse, November 15, 1952 (overtime); 6, Syracuse, at Boston, December 26, 1950

Most Disqualifications, Two Teams: 13, Syracuse 8 at Baltimore 5, November 15, 1952 (overtime); 11, Syracuse 6 at Boston, 5, December 26, 1950

Most Points in a Losing Game: 184, Denver, vs. Detroit at Denver, December 13, 1983 (3 overtimes); 158, Denver, vs. Golden State at Golden State, November 2, 1990
Widest Point Spread: 68, Cleveland 148 vs. Miami 80 at Cleveland, December 17, 1991

Season

Most Games Won: 69, Los Angeles, 1971-72
Most Games Lost: 73, Philadelphia, 1972-73
Longest Winning Streak: 33, Los Angeles, November 5, 1971 to January 7, 1972
Longest Losing Streak: 20, Philadelphia, January 9, 1973 to February 11, 1973; Dallas, November 13, 1993 to December 22, 1993
Most Points Scored: 10,371, Denver, 1981-82
Most Points Allowed: 10,723, Denver, 1990-91
Highest Scoring Average: 126.5, Denver, 1981-82
Highest Average, Points Allowed: 130.8, Denver, 1990-91
Most FG Attempted: 9,295, Boston, 1960-61
Most FG Made: 3,980, Denver, 1981-82
Highest FG Percentage: .545, Los Angeles Lakers, 1984-85
Most FT Attempted: 3,411, Philadelphia, 1966-67
Most FT Made: 2,408, Detroit, 1960-61
Highest FT Percentage: .832, Boston, 1989-90

All-Time NBA Playoff Records

■ ■ ■

Individual

Single Game

Most Points: 63, Michael Jordan, Chicago, at Boston, April 20, 1986 (2 overtimes); 61, Elgin Baylor, Los Angeles, at Boston, April 14, 1962

Most FG Attempted: 48, Wilt Chamberlain, Philadelphia, vs. Syracuse at Philadelphia, March 22, 1962; Rick Barry, San Francisco, vs. Philadelphia at San Francisco, April 18, 1967

Most FG Made: 24, Wilt Chamberlain, Philadelphia, vs. Syracuse at Philadelphia, March 14, 1960; John Havlicek, Boston, vs. Atlanta, at Boston, April 1, 1973; Michael Jordan, Chicago, vs. Cleveland, at Chicago, May 1, 1988

Most 3-Point FG Attempted: 15, Dennis Scott, Orlando, vs. Indiana, May 25, 1995; Nick Van Exel, Los Angeles Lakers, vs. Seattle, May 4, 1995

Most 3-Point FG Made: 8, Dan Majerle, Phoenix, vs. Seattle at Phoenix, June 1, 1993

Most FT Attempted: 32, Bob Cousy, Boston, vs. Syracuse at Boston, March 21, 1953 (4 overtimes); 28, Michael Jordan, Chicago, vs. New York at Chicago, March 14, 1989

Most FT Made: 30, Bob Cousy, Boston, vs. Syracuse at Boston, March 21, 1953 (4 overtimes); 23, Michael Jordan, Chicago, vs. New York at Chicago, March 14, 1989

Most Rebounds: 41, Wilt Chamberlain, Philadelphia, vs. Boston at Philadelphia, April 5, 1967

Most Blocked Shots: 10, Mark Eaton, Utah, vs. Houston at Utah, April 26, 1985; Hakeem Olajuwon, Houston, at Los Angeles Lakers, April 29, 1990

Most Assists: 24, Magic Johnson, L.A. Lakers vs. Phoenix at Los Angeles, May 15, 1984; John Stockton, Utah, at L.A. Lakers, May 17, 1988

Most Steals: 8, done 6 times, most recently by Tim Hardaway, Golden State, at Seattle, April 30, 1992

Most Personal Fouls: 8, Jack Toomay, Baltimore, at New York, March 26, 1949 (overtime)

Team

Single Game

Most Points, One Team: 157, Boston, vs. New York at Boston, April 28, 1990

Most Points, Two Teams: 304, Portland 153 at Phoenix 151, May 11, 1992 (2 overtimes); 285, San Antonio 152 vs. Denver 133 at San Antonio, April 26, 1983; Boston 157 vs. New York 128, at Boston, April 28, 1990

Fewest Points, One Team: 70, Golden State, vs. Los Angeles at Golden State, April 21, 1973; Seattle, at Houston, April 23, 1982

Fewest Points, Two Teams: 145, Fort Wayne 74 vs. Syracuse 71, at Indianapolis, April 7, 1955

Most FG Attempted, One Team: 140, Boston, vs. Syracuse at Boston, March 18, 1959; San Francisco, at Philadelphia, April 14, 1967 (overtime)

Most FG Attempted, Two Teams: 257, Boston 135 vs. Philadelphia 122, at Boston, March 22, 1960

Most FG Made, One Team: 67, Milwaukee, at Philadelphia, March 30, 1970; San Antonio, vs. Denver at San Antonio, May 4, 1983; Los Angeles Lakers, vs. Denver at Los Angeles, May 22, 1985

Most FG Made, Two Teams: 119, Milwaukee 67 at Philadelphia 52, March 30, 1970

Most 3-Point FG Attempted, One Team: 32, Houston, at Orlando, June 7, 1995

Most 3-Point FG Attempted, Two Teams: 62, Houston 32 at Orlando 30, June 7, 1995

Most 3-Point FG Made, One Team: 19, Houston, vs. Utah, April 29, 1995

Most 3-Point FG Made, Two Teams: 28, Houston 19 vs. Utah 9, April 29, 1995

Most FT Attempted, One Team: 70, St. Louis, vs. Minneapolis at St. Louis, March 17, 1956

Most FT Attempted, Two Teams: 128, Syracuse 64 at Boston 64, March 21, 1953 (4 overtimes); 122, St. Louis 70 vs. Minneapolis 52, at St. Louis, March 17, 1956; Minneapolis 68 vs. St. Louis 54, at Minneapolis, March 21, 1956

Most FT Made, One Team: 57, Boston, vs. Syracuse at Boston, March 21, 1953 (4 overtimes); Phoenix, vs. Seattle at Phoenix, June 5, 1993

Most FT Made, Two Teams: 108, Boston 57 vs. Syracuse 51 at Boston, March 21, 1953 (4 overtimes); 91, St. Louis 54 vs. Minneapolis 37 at St. Louis, March 17, 1956

Most Rebounds, One Team: 97, Boston, vs. Philadelphia at Boston, March 19, 1960

Most Rebounds, Two Teams: 169, Boston 89 vs. Philadelphia 80 at Boston, March 22, 1960; San Francisco 93 at Philadelphia 76, April 16, 1967

Most Assists, One Team: 51, San Antonio, vs. Denver at San Antonio, May 4, 1983

Most Assists, Two Teams: 79, Los Angeles Lakers 44 vs. Boston 35, at Los Angeles, June 4, 1987

Most Blocked Shots, One Team: 20, Philadelphia, vs. Milwaukee at Philadelphia, April 5, 1981

Most Blocked Shots, Two Teams: 29, Philadelphia 20 vs. Milwaukee 9, at Philadelphia, April 5, 1981

Most Steals, One Team: 22, Golden State, vs. Seattle at Golden State, April 14, 1975

Most Steals, Two Teams: 35, Golden State 22 vs. Seattle 13, at Golden State, April 14, 1975

Most Personal Fouls, One Team: 55, Syracuse, at Boston, March 21, 1953 (4 overtimes); 45, Syracuse, at New York, April 8, 1952

Most Personal Fouls, Two Teams: 106, Syracuse 55 at Boston 51, March 21, 1953 (4 overtimes); 82, Syracuse 45 at New York 37, April 8, 1952

Most Disqualifications, One Team: 7, Syracuse, at Boston, March 21, 1953 (4 overtimes)

Most Disqualifications, Two Teams: 12, Syracuse 7 at Boston 5, March 21, 1953 (4 overtimes); 7, Los Angeles 4 at Detroit 3, April 3, 1962

Widest Point Spread: 58, Minneapolis 133 vs. St. Louis 75, at Minneapolis, March 19, 1956

Who's Calling the Shots?

1-f, 2-d, 3-a, 4-b, 5-g, 6-e, 7-c

Who's Who in Scoring

1-c, 2-f, 3-a, 4-j, 5-b, 6-i, 7-h, 8-e, 9-g, 10-d

The College Connection

1-e, 2-i, 3-f, 4-a, 5-c, 6-j, 7-g, 8-d, 9-h, 10-b

Know Your Colors

1-i, 2-e, 3-a, 4-h, 5-j, 6-c, 7-f, 8-d, 9-g, 10-b

There's No Place Like Home

1-i, 2-f, 3-l, 4-e, 5-k, 6-g, 7-b, 8-j, 9-h, 10-d, 11-a, 12-c

```
F R E Y R R O H G T P P M
O I D M O G F C I T O N A
L L G E N C R N S O U R L
K G A I A F X P I C N U O
C G W J S T A R K S U B N
E L A U E P A C R G H E
L I M K E W E P U N I S H
Y N Y A G E O X I L V A N
A W M A L S E N L O A M O
L P O P W B N L A C G X O
B E L O V A N D U K E M P
N O R N M A D E C D E R S
A D N E W I F R R I D E R
D A R F K O N E A L E F E
R P E E O F O B T H E S H
O R L E X E N A V R C B T
J I L A R L B D R I D W A
U C I G W I E Y I N W X E
P E M Y E L K R A B C E W
```

LEARN TO PLAY BASKETBALL
THE NBA WAY!

With This Electrifying, Grab-a-Ball-and-Try-It Guide

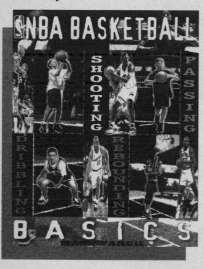

- Exciting, full-color photographs of the stars in action.

- Drills, tips, and suggestions from some of the greatest players and coaches of all time.

- Techniques for dribbling, shooting, rebounding, passing, defending, and more.

- Fantastic how-to photos of boys and girls in NBA-run training sessions.

128 pages (all in color), 8 x 10, Paper 0-8069-0928-5 $9.95

All-time greats like Larry Bird, John Stockton, Michael Jordan, Tim Hardaway, and Kareem Abdul-Jabbar will help you get on your way to becoming a superstar!

Available in fine stores everywhere.

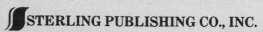

STERLING PUBLISHING CO., INC.